REMEMBER
WHO
YOU ARE

THE AWAKENING

To Kathy
Namaste'
David Porter

Printed in United States of America
New Life Publications First Printing: February 1998
Second Printing: September 1998

ISBN: 0-9660386-0-6
Library of Congress Catalog Card Number 97-92832

ILLUSTRATIONS & COVER DESIGN
(Painted Freehand)
BY LANA CHANDA

New Life Publications
PO Box 3632
Sedona, AZ 86340
(520) 204-9204

CONTENTS

ACKNOWLEDGMENTS

Vicki Margaritis for her understanding guidance and unending support.

Barbara Colgan for all her love and counsel of the wise.

Lana Chanda for my first experience in unconditional love and the tremendous help and inspiration in this book.

Nancy Akca—With Nancy's enduring tenacity, you are now able to receive the messages herein.

Sharon Jefferies, my favorite real hu-woman. Thank you for your support.

Pat Sumstine of "My Imagination" for her design and editing contributions. Thank you Pat for your outstanding instruction.

Anne Lary—Thank you so much Anne for your assistance and support.

Heather Lary—Thanks for your efficiency.

MANUAL FOR THE NEW ERA

A must-read for those living under the influence of the opinions of others.

- More powerful than man's rules and laws.

- Assisting in removal of emotional mountains.

- Has information you won't find in tall buildings.

- More likely to be cited than an off-duty officer caught speeding.

Written for the benefit of my race—the one I believe in or why would I be here—the human race, but it's okay if ET's read it; hope they understand earth humor.

COMING SOON
Remember Who You Are, Volume 2

INTRODUCTION

By the title of this book, you may have already picked up on what is meant in this introduction when I say, "We will be introducing you to You in these writings." Kind of like self meeting self, or outer self meeting inner self would be more accurate. There is much conjecture about "Self." You have heard the opinions all of your life about "the self," but have they brought you self-realization?

In the chapters to come, there will be cases in which I give myself as the living example of the experiences I exclaim. I will share with you the reasons I no longer call myself names like: "I'm sorry," or what I have heard from many lips, "I'm terribly sorry," "I'm unworthy," "dead tired," "pretty stupid," or "I'm such an idiot," etc. Nor do I go through life any longer justifying my actions, or lack thereof, or living in a state of excuse-idis over what some perceive as my imperfections. As far as living in the so-common-of-all states, "self denial," we will reflect upon this one, yes?

As I am not interested in impressing the sophisticated intellect who feels the need to be impressed by how one writes, rather than what one is expressing in the message, you should find this book quite easy to follow because I just happen to be one o' them down-home kinda' guys and I write in a down-home kinda way. I've read books with such grandiose linguistic terminology and intricate topologies, not to mention, such a seeming need from the writer for a dramatic stimulus in verbiage as to place self on the highest-of-all-form writing pedestals. Even Mr. Webster would need his dictionary to follow along. Ralph Waldo Emerson himself, would be in awe attempting to assimilate, elucidate and conceptualize the intensity of verbal articulation of some of the books into which I have delved. I wish my message to be so simple that even the very young may comprehend it. They are indeed entitled to it as well as any. I will not be bearing any apologies to the religious sector of this planet for my sometimes direct layman verbiage. It was the negative "control freak" attitudes of religions that initiated my profound interest in the research of their belief systems and structures, so as to discover why and how people belonging to them would literally force their organized institutionalized convictions and concepts of belief down my throat and force me to be baptized, and to memorize the Book the pastors thump. I have two statements for them:

FIRST: I would like to say, "Thank you," because now when someone says to me, "It is all in THE BOOK, read the Book," as they refer to the Bible, of course; I can say, "I have not only read the Book, but researched it. I know why it has existed for so long, and how it came about."

I have also studied many books of the Bible's origin—including *The Lost Books of the Bible*—some of which will be in my next book, and some of which many humans are not even close to being ready for.

SECOND: I have one word for Religion, and that is the word it comes from the Latin word, "Religio," which translates in its original language, not English—thank God—to "TO UNITE." Those influencing others through their religious beliefs would do well in the converting practice if they themselves would convert to apply the understanding of the true meaning of this misused word.

God, that felt good! Stay tuned, there will be plenty more elevational perception clarification of past traditions that will stimulate anyone, but blow the socks off the skimmerbugs who desire to control this area of the Milky Way, this planet, their spouses or employees. For the most fitting of titles for these bullish attitudes, I will be using the term, "control freaks."

On this beautiful planet, there are thousands who control billions. Because of that control, they pad their pockets well and can afford protection for whatever they do. You all saw the O.J. trial. You know exactly what I mean; "Money answers all things."

Yes, I told you I read THE BOOK. If you wish to validate that statement, then look up the word "thing" in your Webster. This book is just one of the wake-up calls to the billions who have played as zombies, robots and slaves to the thousands. When there are no wars, many factories have no demand for their products—some of these are where many of you punch time-cards. They have you seemingly in a catch-22 position. There is a better way than to work with, and for, the ones who are polluting and destroying this delicate, sensitive, beautiful, but powerful planet.

By the time this book is out, you will have sensed some more samples of our planet's power. Burying garbage in her wounds is going to cause her to cough, sneeze, and scratch her face. We are in for major lessons on how to treat a lady larger than all of us put together by several trillion, trillion times.

Earth is going into a higher vibrational frequency and if you care to join her, you must raise yours too. That is what this book is all about. So, if the enlightenments herein seem to get under your skin, you might ask yourself, "What's under there?"

It is your choice to investigate your personal belief systems so as to uncover any old patterns that may not serve your best interests on your potential path to enlightenment. If you have "RED" buttons, ask Self, "Why?" I do not convert you, I share. I only have my truth— you have yours. It is your choice to understand negativity in your emotional content. Ignoring problems does not make them go away. Understanding negatives stimulated by their leader, "FEAR," is a prerequisite for at-one-ment into higher levels of heavenly states of awareness.

The process is Embracement my beloved earth brothers and sisters. It is time, on all of our calendars of events for super-consciousness; however, it is not mandatory. Those who continue to believe in two Gods will simply not get it. You know, one big wrathful one— up there, the other one with horns—down there.

Now for a most educational journey into the human aura and what it reveals about you and your neighbors. I have selected, from over 10,000 cases, the ones that made the most lasting impressions on me, as examples for you. They should impress your memory with which color represents which attitudes and characteristics, etc., so as to leave a lasting impression for your instant recall as you begin to invoke your auric sight.

As you will see, these writings are to invoke more in you than auric vision—with your acceptance, they will. I cannot make you one with everything, but will remind you that you already are.

So be it.

FOREWORD

There is more to you than meets the eye, most eyes anyway. More precisely, there is much that meets the eye that does not register to the brain or screen of the mind for viewing.

As a matter of electromagnetic fact, there is an energy field in color around all animate and inanimate atomic structures. By repeated invocation and continual awareness that these energy fields are there, you will reawaken deep, hidden memories and begin to view them. A very powerful tool that you can employ for results in viewing this energy field is a simple childlike belief.

As we enter this course in awakening, you will be given great detail in animating these and other gifts yet dormant in you because we, as earthly incarnates, have been descending from light for let's say, "so long," we have experienced major memory shutdown. This has caused the veil effect over the true spirit beings that we are, and has limited our abilities to use the tremendous spiritual gifts we have always possessed. I will add here, that the institutional structures have not been excessively beneficial in us li'l earthean's awakening to our spiritual inheritance.

Many are now becoming aware that our scientists have invented ways in which to photograph the human aura. In many areas you can now go to a local metaphysical bookstore and get an instant photo of your aura. If they are not equipped with an aura camera, they should know where to find one. Your local psychic fairs and wholistic expos normally have at least one aura photographer.

So now you won't ever be inclined to open your personal auric sight, right? I think other! I believe as aura-imaging photography grows around the globe, as it is now doing, it will inspire memory in us all—memory that we already have, the ability to view auric fields. I own one of these aura photo cameras and have experimented extensively with it. I set the camera up at a therapeutic clinic I had in Scottsdale, Arizona for a time and tracked the auras of my clients to assist in evaluating their progress from the different therapies given.

In my own personal skepticism of this technology, I have tested the accuracy hundreds of times. I have discovered the camera is not as accurate as the eye on photographing the aura, but comes in second place with excellent accuracy. In the chapters that follow, I will explain this electromagnetic field we call the aura in vivid detail. Why it is there, from where it comes, what it has to do with you and most of all, how you can recondition your body, mind, and life as you brighten your aura and vice-versa.

I will give instruction to the reader on how to reawaken this dormant insight. Auric fields have always been with us. They need not remain an invisible part of your life or sight any longer.

Along with expanding your level of awareness to this insight, similar attitudes of adjustment will open you to amazing new areas of consciousness.

Some most important educational enlightenments imbedded in these writings are:

ONE, that one special day will arrive for each and every human who has an "opening of the mind" to see the human auras around their family and friends and all others.

Familiarizing yourself with the meaning of the colors around people, how they got there, and how to change them to the more useful and preferred, will put you a step ahead of the new foundations and institutions that will begin to spring up as demand for them increases. Many who obtain this information just prior to ground floor opening of opportunities will be the ones administrating and teaching the neophytes who will be acquiring this sight.

TWO: Won't it be just downright time-saving to know, through the one you're dealing with by the viewing of his auric colors, whether or not that used car, piece of land, or investment is truly, by his opinion, an honest deal? Of course, if you happen to be dealing with an unreliable person, he won't know how you know because the vibrations of a liar will not allow them the higher insights. Imagine a scam-free planet and imagine it vividly because that is what will bring it into your reality. Do you see that in authoring such material, all the dishonest people of the planet may not be too thrilled about me, to include the ones in high places? When it comes voting time, they will wonder how on earth the poles could possibly slip so far against them that their only votes came from family members.

Your auric sight, with understanding of the shades, will set you above the technology of the polygraph.

THREE: You won't wonder if someone likes you when you see a pink cloud leave them headed for you. Not to mention all that I am about to mention.

CHAPTER 1

Thoughts Are Real Things

"All that we are is a result of what we have thought. The mind is everything. What we think, we become."

- BUDDHA

"If we could see our thoughts go out upon the ethers gathering more and more of their kind, and return, we would not only be amazed at what we give birth to, but would scream for deliverance."

When thought is initiated, it simultaneously and instantaneously molds light into energy; which in turn seeks to become the nature of its intent in third dimensional form or activity. Keep in mind that there is plenty of room in your, let's say— hard drive—for new thoughts that create new programs. Also important to know, thoughts will appear in your mind even if you are not the initiator. It will behoove you to *become* the initiator, and not just the recipient.

Honorable lesson number one on how to initiate thought: "BE STILL!" Thoughts, although invisible to the eye, are real living things. Air is also invisible, but it is still there, isn't it? Imagine if you had to believe in air to have it! Some believe God is invisible, does it mean He isn't there? I offer that you can "loose" the idea of God being invisible; only the higher than third dimension is invisible to most. The rest of God is quite easily gazed upon. For anything you can identify in the illusions of your mind you perceive as NOT GOD, I would refer you to the most thumped book of them all, which so plainly states, "God is All, All is One."

As we go into the next area of content, you may begin to feel a slight sensation one inch behind and above the right ear, which is referred to as Hanger 39, excuse me Area 39, the physical area that stimulates the memory. OOPS, now you might have thoughts of ET's and of course they aren't for real—at least if you haven't seen them, huh?, which brings us to a short, true story.

I was not skeptical about the stories of UFOs' that I heard from time to time as a young man, just eager to see one myself. Well, long about the age of 17 it was Army time for David. After basic training and A.I.T., I was stationed at Ft. Bliss, Texas, a military base of missiles, for one thing.

The year was 1971. The time was night time, about 2 a.m. I was in a jeep headed out to a very large ammunition dump (storage area). I didn't know what I was guarding, but I met someone that I believed did know; and I don't mean the Lieutenant or Sergeant of the guard, who were both in the jeep with me.

You see, it was actually my turn to be asleep back in the guard shack or barracks. However, there was a round of ammo missing and I didn't know they counted that stuff. For you animal lovers, I swear I didn't shoot anything alive.

Hey, it's quite boring walking around miles of fenced-in desert, guarding stuff which its purpose is to kill. As we were kicking around in the brush for the "lost" round of ammo, myself and eight others, it was so quiet that we could hear the lizards running through the brush and sand—so silent you could literally hear the drop of a pin.

As I stopped and noticed some other guards beside me looking up, I too turned and looked that direction and SAW...

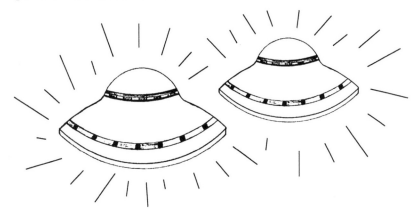

...THIS in the dark sky above; two of the most illuminated "whatever" you wish to label them. Not one sound, even as one, then later the other, left our viewing range. I will never forget the first one that flew away from us. It was so fast that, had we been counting by seconds when it began to get smaller, we would have made it to about 2.5 seconds before we could no longer see it. The other craft made like a slow motion pinball before dismissing its awesome presence.

Something you might find amusing is that I already knew I was in trouble with the earth Army and I would have been delighted to hitchhike outta there with the ET's at the time. The military and I didn't seem to have similar interests or compatible ideas. I departed as a Private the same as I'd arrived. If you think I'm proud of that, your perception is clear. I received no penalties after our experience.

Over the next two days, many others, both on and off base, had a lot of paperwork pile up on their desk—which was then safely tucked away. Funny thing, after the excitement—it seemed it was only us Privates who saw anything. To all the Sergeants and officers, these beautiful craft became an invisible anomaly.

What I saw were two ships, approximately 40-60 feet across, maybe 15-20 feet from top to bottom, metallic with a golden, luminous glow. They made absolutely no noise.

The reason I share this true story is a principle to keep in mind; "Just because it's invisible don't mean it ain't there!"

There is something else that over time and much programming of denial and memory loss, has become invisible to many an eye—the electromagnetic field we call "aura." Each and every vibration causes an effect, the effect is in color. Each effect is a specific color according to the vibration that caused it. The vibration is the exact reflection of the nature of the thought that created the vibration, that caused the friction in the atmosphere, that brings that shade of color for the viewing. Rather than "stomping out" on me here, keep reading. This concept will be paraphrased.

I have read in science books which, as you know, get some major updates periodically, that the human is made up of a lotta cells. One reference says six trillion, so let's go with that one for the 90's. Now in these cells that construct your body, you gotta whole lot of molecules and atoms which are what you might call pretty empty. They say 99.999% empty; so in my calculation, there is plenty of room to put stuff in 'em.

Now instead of making you guess, here's some of the stuff in the atom, beginning with the largest. First, as we go into the atom, there is the electron, nucleus, neutron, proton, ozone, bozone, photon, quarks; particles three. You won't find reference to these three particles in your science books as of 1997. These particles are what carry light, as we call it, into the cells. You may direct these particles with your own personal, individual free will of mind and thought power. Need I go deeper? Please allow me.

You may call these particles any name you choose, sticks and stones won't affect them either. Prana, Chi, Monadic Essence, Holy Spirit, Daily Bread or Spiritual Nourishment. Select your favorite title and feel free to change it at any earth time so desired. The name of the energy is not our goal of teaching.

Science research has proven the molecules that make matter become solid actually do respond to thought.

One of the seminar titles in the workshops I provide for humans, is "Into the Light." It is said this way, "Light is the cause and effect of itself." It is always available for your personal use. You may use as much as you THINK you can. If you used as much as all humans who have ever walked the planet, you would not deplete as much as the energy it takes for the mite on the flea to clip his toenail, because light, like silly putty, is into reform. You have the right to reshape light all day long. When you intend—that's called thought—you just used light. Every aspect of the light you use returns unto itself when you've finished playing with it.

You may have heard a statement like, "I think he's using her" or

"She's using him." Imagine buying the most comfortable, best look-ing pair of shoes you have ever owned and after trying them on at the shoe store, you put them away and never wear them again, so as to never wear them out.

It's a contract of the souls to use one another and it's a deal you can refuse—but no worry mate—you'll get another chance later, again and again and again, even though it is another person, it is in es-sence, source using source. One thing you cannot use too much of is everything or the ALL.

When you originate thought, you manifest energy. The energy then has the nature of the intent of the thought or thinker and fol-lows the thought wherever it leads. The intent is the program of the thought. It has been given purpose; therefore, goes out and magne-tizes to like thoughts, so as to bring into being its original intent. Its soul purpose is to become the activity, idea or solid matter of the intent of the sender, originator or creator. The energy is slave to the thought and the light just goes along for the ride. There is much more to thought than one might think, but that's another book.

When thought manipulates light, the light decreases in vibration causing variations of the many choices of colors according to the nature of the intent.

In later chapters, we go into specific detail of the different shades and their meanings with personal real-life stories to assist you in knowing the meaning of each shade. So as you begin to break loose from the old fear-invoked conditionings of the past, you can and will begin to view the new Golden Age, Era, Times (choose favorite title) in living multicolor.

That age is here now; are you enjoying it? Besides the sheer beauty around everything; imagine buying a house, automobile or land without a paper contract; not to mention, as you see thought (intentions in living color); you will become aware there is even more to you yet to be used. For those who are focused on job security, that's just the old conditioned thinking of lack, want and limitation. The jobs and careers of the new age will sustain ample abundance and a great deal more enjoyment in life.

If one lives in fear-based thoughts, which truly are the basis of all negativity, they are impregnating themselves with lower vibrations which are represented in color. The more materialistic nature colors such as yellow, orange, down in order to red are not to be confused with negativity, but simply thoughts of different aspirations. It is when they get mixed, cloudy or muddy that they, for the most part, represent negative thought. Every shade of color has its own unique blueprint of meaning.

I was in Springfield, Missouri, at a small bookstore called Celestial Horizons one day with my aura camera, taking pictures of people and then explaining the meaning of the colors in their auric field. I thought I had the color meaning down pretty well—then I got a little lesson in my personal development course in guessology.

A young lady stepped up for a photo. I peeled the back off the Polaroid film and saw—to my amazement—a huge cloud of the most pure, bright "cotton candy" pink I'd ever seen around a human. The young lady knew not what the color meant, but was most excited about its beauty.

Well, let me tell ya, it was just too simple for ol' Colombo here, as

I viewed that wedding band on her left hand. "Just got married, huh?" I said.

A stillness came over the room, as ones who knew her were standin' close by.

She looked up with an expression of, "What are you talkin' about dude?" and said, "I've been married three years."

Somehow I picked up that it was not necessarily an affectionate three years. I was aware of the statistical fact that three is the most common cycle of divorce. I then went in just a li'l deeper, by blurting, "Well, pink represents affection so this shows someone you are very affectionate towards."

She replied, "If you mean my husband, guess again." Now how was I to know her husband drank, smoked, chewed, cussed and exemplified as a big, bad, mean, control freak?

At about that point, one of her friends took me to the side and enlightened me about the matter. Somehow I had the flashback of Forest Gump saying, "Stupid is as Stupid does."

She stepped over, looking up to me as a distinct sparkle began to emit from her eyes and said, "Could it be all pink like that 'cause I got a li'l baby kitten yesterday?"

That hit me like cotton candy in the face. How on earth could I be gullible enough to think that kind of affection would exist between two humans of the opposite sex, married in the 90's?

I went on to explain her other colors and how the more affection—towards or from someone or some thing—that more pink will be in the aura. The more pure and original the pink, the more pure and original the affection. Not often do I see such a pastel pink around the human. When I do, it often represents their affection toward a puppy or kitten.

A brighter, fairly pure pink usually surrounded by red may represent the affection towards, or from a baby, small child, or more often, grandchild.

The affection between lovers and lovers-to-be is seldom, and I mean seldom, a pastel or cotton candy shade of pink. This is due to the intent and emotions involved. The pink gives way to more of a red mixture causing a bright shade of magenta, representing a bright emotional "turn on." The more sensual the attraction, the more red or scarlet mixture, causing a burgundy shade. If that burgundy is pure and bright, you can graduate the sensual to sexual attraction, or just figure that the person with the burgundy is simply downright "in the mood for you to be in the nude"—if ya know what I mean. I suppose these aura cameras could find a whole new meaning for marketing, if at this point I said "dating service."

If you see a muddy red or burgundy, blackish or brownish red, you are viewing attitudes of—pick one—control, manipulation, fear, guilt, shame, pressure from a lover, mate, spouse, parent or child to parent, etc. It is a very low or negative energy in the nature of the minds that emit, transmit or receive it, no matter who the role players are.

Red is a powerful color, but no more negative than any other. It is the muddy shades that represent attitudes of selfishness, jealousy, envy, resentment, remorse, hostility, anger, and the like. These less-than-bright shades of color, stem from the less-than-bright shades of intent, emotion, attitude, and thought.

Be a responder. Embrace and release the old reactor. It is not color that is negative or positive, but the way in which you apply your energies. The color is just the reflection of your reaction or response of your reception. All negative action, reaction, activities, concepts, feelings, patterns and programs of any kind have a foundation— FEAR.

When you see someone judging the other, they have fear. If their life seems to be fear-based, you can "bet your sweet bippy" it was planted there by some well-meaning organization that seeks to control the li'l sheep with fear of that two-horned varmit who lives down under, awaiting your life in damnation, or the other one—you know— the wrathful one awaiting your sentencing and punishment.

What's ol' Lucifer gonna do, make a big army of little devils and invade heaven, dethrone God and set everything on fire? God forbid. I don't foresee God being dethroned.

When I went into the aura photography business, I lived in Nixa, Missouri. I booked myself and the camera to go to metaphysical bookstores, fairs, groups, and just about anywhere anyone would have me. Well, I didn't know the people who visit Branson, Missouri would react to my camera like it was some kinda' black magic. I mean, science has been working on this Electromagnetic Field Imaging Photography for longer than any of them are old.

I owned an office supply company in Nixa, just up the road a piece from Branson and I got to know some of the people down there who used my products and services. One of them, a theater owner , allowed me to set up my camera in his theater. I discovered many of his customers are scared to death of life. Let me explain.

I said the word, "astrology" to a full-grown woman and she cringed as she said, "Ain't that the work of the devil?"

I said, "I don't work with him. Where did you study astrology?"

She replied, "I didn't study that."

I asked, "How can you judge it?" Then I asked, "Have you been going to Faith Baptist Church? I know what they teach—I was raised in it."

She said, "Yes, since my husband passed away."

One lady came up to my display board looking at all the examples of previous aura photos. I politely rose and said, "Them's auras."

She grabbed her purse as she initiated the ol' double-time march saying, "Oh, I don't believe in them things!"

I said, "But yours is following you!"

At about that time, a big ol' cowboy stepped up to protect that poor ol' gal and said, "You want me to tell you what I think of that kinda stuff?" Well, I'd already been there for two days and except for the employees who worked at the theater, only one brave soul would dare to sit for a photo so I could shine a light on her thoughts.

So I answered the ol' boy and said, "Yes sir, I would be most interested in any input, information or feedback you could give me on the electromagnetic field called the human aura.

"You know that since as far back as 1890, science has been experimenting with it. In the 40's, the Soviet scientists, Semyon and his spouse, Valentina Kirlian, made great advancements in their research to provide us with a very accurate biofeedback method in which we can detect health disorders. You may have heard of Kirlian Photography? A good example of what the different shades represent would be; pink, showing an individual's affection, compassion and understanding toward all the human race we live with here on this wonderful planet." I went on with an in-depth explanation of the human auric field, then said, "What were you gonna share about the aura?"

You know, that ol' boy never did tell me what he thought of "that kinda' stuff." He used five words through the duration of our conversation and they were, "Oh yeah," and, "Is that right?" He did intone them several times though. I was glad I could share, with at least that one fella', and now don't ya' know that fella' knows more about them aura things than most anyone in that whole territory? I'll bet he told all his friends about Kirlian Photography.

I relate this story, all of it true to the word to inform you on an activity that has been taking place on your planet. Humans hear this: The people, places, and organizations are not important to the principle of what their control over you has caused, that being FEAR. With it, they have manipulated you into believing they have your answer and they will always say it is in THE BOOK! Don't you see? They read the parts they want you to hear, then explain it in the way they want you to understand. If they can manipulate you, they can control you. As long as they control you, you will serve their purpose, rather than your own. If human slavery was still accepted by "us," "they" would continue to use it as an easy means to get what they want out of "you." Not long ago this attitude was legal by "man's" law, was it not?

Look at the trillions of your dollars it took to establish the worldwide organizations/institutions/religions which could be, and someday may be, a wonderful thing if it weren't done for selfish motives and calling you sinners, scaring the hell *into* you, not *out* of you. …then they pass the plate.

If my words sound like judgment, so be it. Know this winners— sinners, you are not; I judge the latitude of attitude. I judge the setting of the thermostat of the mind, as it were, and the attitudes that set the stats; minds. I love them as well as I love this gorgeous Goddess, Mother Earth. They truly know not what they do. If you choose to come home, that is the beginning of acceptance of love and light, rather than the oh-so-long-deep-seeded patterns, traditions, and hand-downs of the psychologies of dogma.

You may now repossess your personal God-given powers. "I beseech ye brethren to use your soul's power—gifts of the soul" or you shall remain with the same thought, same vibration, same color, SAME LIFE!

No one can reset your thermostat (mind). You must do it yourself. Take charge of your own thinking and begin to see yourself shift from the plateau of consciousness you now view earth life from, to levels of awareness, which most believe are only possible after disembodiment.

In the next chapter, we will explain that pure thought means single thought. Later, we will give you instructions on how to bring your mind into single focus.

Remember Who You Are

Pure Thought
Pure Color
Pure Cure

"All I want to know are the thoughts of God,
all else is a footnote."

- ALBERT EINSTEIN

The mind does not function on the reverse of a negative idea. When one states, for example, "I want to quit smoking," the subconscious mind may only assimilate the "want smoking." Contemplate that for a moment of your earth time while I add the next example, "I want to, or will, lose weight." Next example, "I've got to quit drinking or drugs." Your subconscious mind is working *for* you—not against you, but just as in the best of all computers, what you program in will do the retrieving—no big favor if it is initially programmed in confusion.

Your subconscious mind is out to protect you, even from yourself. It doesn't want you to quit, lose, or stop anything and knows that you don't "got" to do anything.

Remember it has been designed by God for a freewill carrier. This is the reverse of the conceptual idea, on which your subconscious mind doesn't function. It knows in truth that all you want to do is move forward in growth and knows no other direction. The negative ideas come in because of our previous conditioning—being smaller or larger in structure, or having abnormal physical appearance, skin color, etc. Our subconscious mind has already recorded these conditions as negative in aspect.

Also important to know, a statement made in the past or future tense will automatically cancel itself out, as it is being stated, whether positive or negative in origin. Such affirmations are as the seed planted atop the sandy, windy desert. To affect any change in preconditioned programs or to create anew, you must always state the desired results clearly and in the present tense.

"Moral" is wonderful, but not what is meant in this chapter when I say "pure." Pure thought indicates single thought, which provides the thinker to be in clear focus of the desire. If your thoughts are characterized in negativity, clutter, hurry, worry, unclear, or off focus, the auric field around you will display this. Attempts to create cure or assistance becomes as ineffective as the mixed and confused thoughts that originate the impurities of color. There is great personal power in the learning of how to focus in the now with pure thought.

True story: Once there was a young man changing his tire on an automobile. The jack gave way with him under the car. His mother was with him and the only one there for miles around. She had no time for any thought except "ONE!" Like Paul Harvey would say, "and you know the rest of the story."

I would have liked to view the screen of that mother's mind when the car fell on her boy. I will guarantee you there was only one precise thought on that screen and it must have viewed something like this:

THIS
CAR
GOING
UP ! !

I trust I have drawn a clear picture of the power of pure and positive thought!

It is true that the athlete breathes more and breathes deeper than the average bearer of a physical body and that ain't no boo-boo. Another thing the athlete does is move the muscles, joints, and all the little pieces and parts of the body more than the average non-athlete. There is yet another factor to consider. Why it is that the trained athlete is much more likely to reach their set goal than the non-athlete?

Have you ever looked up the word "plumline" in the dictionary? I have, but here is my personal definition.

PLUMLINE: The direct, concentrated, clear, pure, singular, unencumbered focus of the hawk in flight at the sighting of dinner on the ground 'long about meal time.

Everything on that bird's body is on full automatic pilot as the body pauses in midair, wings flapping on automatic, the 'plumline,' focus on the meal below with one conscious thought...

TAG YOU'RE IT!

Again, I wisheth that I have drawn an appropriate picture in your mind as to how the mind of concentration will more likely reach any goal, intent or desire than the unclear or unfocused.

At this point, of course, if your thoughts are, "How do I get focused mind power too?" I will answer that now, if you skip pages after I do, you may miss some of the basis of our message to you. Yoga, Zen, Zar, Transcendental Meditations, Middle Eastern philosophies, etc., are all great at assisting you in the process known as baptism of the mind and the activity of repenting of the mind.

In the final chapters, we include the art of meditation in several choices, forms, and methods, and also explain the original meanings of such words as baptize, repent, and forgive from the original Aramaic language from whence they originated.

Many masters have come to earth in an attempt to help us re-awaken to our higher gifts, but we have made it an exceptionally difficult job for them. I mean, do you know what it's like when you're giving a group talk and every time you get to the most enlightening part of your speech, some of the listeners have such a fear that God's gonna' come from the sky and throw them all in hell for blasphemy. They haven't the foggiest idea the guy they are casting the stones at is GOD? "If you have seen me, you have seen the Father."

Mind you here, I judge the activity stimulated by fear from igno-rance; not the stone casters, if you happen to be one. If you are liv-ing in fear, as long as you say, "But I can't help it, I don't know what to do about it," you're right! So maybe you won't hear this. Give what you fear a love thrashing and witness the vaporizing power of love.

Your subconscious mind is extremely sensitive and therefore may be reprogrammed, just as it has been initially programmed. How-ever, it can only record for playback what it understands. When your statements are, "I want to have a slim body," "I wish to be rich," "I would like to quit smoking," "I am getting healthy," your subcon-scious mind understands that you would like to acquire these condi-tions later, but you do not have them now.

The problem here is, the subconscious mind functions only in the present tense. It simply does not know anything about later, ex-cept that which you affirm in future tense is something you do not accept in the present. The subconscious mind is the most sensitive instrument in the universe. It does not discriminate. It records everything fed into it with 100% accuracy and memory. Yes, you can make it believe anything, even a lie, oh yeah! You say, "Well I'm a li'l Miss Goodie, I wouldn't tell a lie." I may challenge that, but your subconscious mind has been with you all your life and it won't challenge or deny anything. Do you think it has never been lied to? It has heard and recorded you being called all kinds of things like sinner, shameful, unworthy, etc. At any time you did not consciously override or chose, at the time of input, not to accept the information being fed to you, your subconscious mind automatically put it on your floppy disc and it became your truth, even if it was a lie.

It is important for you to know you have already been misprogrammed or you just won't want to do anything about it. One must realize they are in prison if they are to be motivated to escape.

Here is a straightforward defamation the subconscious mind understands quite well, "Lord, I AM unworthy." If God is an indoor kinda' guy and your body is His temple, through which He desires to express life, why in His name would you call yourself names like that?

Now if you were to specify by saying, "Lord or Higher Mind, I, the lower body or actually four lower bodies of alter ego, by right of free-will, am unworthy," you would be closer to the truth. However, Mother Earth may be saddened by the insult toward the body she loaned you.

The way to change the world is to change *your* world. The power of your words is one of three major avenues you can use. However, until you step out of self-judgment and judgment of others, you won't be able to live in and apply the needed energies to affect the affirmations and words that bring one into the higher vibrations of love necessary for personal transformation.

There are so many human beings walking around this planet asking that ol' famous question of separation, "Are you a Christian?" You can bet they have backup, and plenty of it, by some religious order, on defining what this label represents. OOPS! Now you went too far David, I suppose now you think you are the reincarnation of King David and can get away with this kind of thought-provoking inquiry, huh? Sure that's possible, why not? I've been around. I don't believe God is limited in any way. I believe in eternity. Now if you assume that I am knocking religion, you are following along pretty well. Jesus did not come to start a religion. There was already enough of that here. It was the religious sector that sought His demise. The "good" religious sector today can justify all their ways and many say, "But that is why Jesus came, so that He could be taken up that hill for capital punishment, so we could be saved from our sins." Don't be coy, that was just one more sin out of FEAR. Many people take comfort knowing Jesus indicated that they are just unaware. "They know not what they do." I mean, I can certainly empathize with their guilt.

In the study of THE BOOK, Jesus said, "I and my Father are one." Imagine that, hanging GOD on a cross to die! I can understand, on a third dimensional level, how one may feel shame for such an injustice. It is no wonder that the acceptance of reincarnation is not very popular amongst the proclaimed Christians. You see, along with this belief system, someone—and there were plenty of them—would have to admit to throwing those stones at Jesus and assisting in His Lynching.

Imagine that! Some of us, here now, did that dastardly deed. It wasn't you was it? Someone did it. I mean why are we poppin' up out here 2,000 years later anyway? Maybe you'll keep poppin' up until you learn to love God and all of her creation.

Religion means to unite, not to separate into groups where each believes theirs is going to heaven and yours is not. They are the chosen few, you are not! They know God, you do not. They inherit the earth, you do not. These havoc-causing attitudes have stimulated mass consciousness into the concept called separateness. Any part of God you think you are not, will not shine through you. Until the "now moment" of pure, clear focus is used by the focuser to loose these conditions, attitudes, and belief systems that have been deeply programmed into the cellular structure you are, you won't be able to get it!

Know that your garden of thoughts (mind body), will begin to grow new and different fruit, as you begin to plant new and different seeds. You must plant first, rid the old weeds in your mind body by using positive statements in the present tense, such as, "From the Lord God of my being, I call forth the all consuming violet fire to release me from all undesired negative conditions and programs, annihilating them core record memory cause and effect; past, present and future. Thank you." Then go forward toward life in low gear and learn the process of giving thanks in all things, savor every now moment.

Fall gently into the attitude of being in love with your universe. Ask not what it can do for you, make love to it, all of it, all your love. Clean out your closet by infiltrating it with statements, words and affirmations that create peace, love, abundance, and harmony. Know in your heart and mind, with the trust and faith of an infant, that the infinite hears every word and thought and is doing its own thinking, along with you, according to yours.

Yes, God is inside, thinking, "Oh boy, I finally get to go out and play through means of one more part; spark, child I am."

As you apply these rewarding new attitudes, realize the new energies working in and around you are in color, more pure and brighter colors. As this purging process is underway, keep the momentum going by embracing each now moment, no matter how depressing, hostile or negative it may seem. Embrace it and give thanks for it; it is just part of the process of awakening to the higher vibrations.

As your moments of doubt arise, and certainly just as the farmer awaits his crops knows they will; the hot, dry sun, the rains and floods, the IRS., they all come to you for the testing as need be. Embrace them all, thank them all. In the middle of the storms, pause, put it in neutral, take a deep breath, "be still" and know God is enjoying the experience right along with you, and made it just for you. Catered for every need, want, and desire to be fulfilled.

Ralph Waldo Emerson said, "You will have what you give your energy to." The meaning here; if you resist fear, you increase fear. Don't empower negativity by focusing on how bad it is. Embrace it and stand upright and watch it dissolve back into the pool of allness. Remember how Jesus put it? He said, "You can't handle that baggage. Put it on my shoulders, that is what I am here for." Don't think for a moment that guy is not here, just because you haven't seen

Him in your neighborhood on roller blades. I do not recall any information on body parts found in the tomb where they placed Jesus, only clothes. The last verse in Matthew states, "I am with you alway, even unto the end of the world."

Know that your thoughts are real things and like all thoughts, are just as contagious as any others. Be in your precious gift, the now moment, in charge of your thinking. Are you thinking, "Are my thoughts worth catching?" Well, you're gonna' catch 'em, so I hope so. My thoughts, you're thoughts, all thoughts, are magnetized to you simply by your focusing upon them.

This universe you're part of works in a circular motion, God's favorite number "0." Everything you energize by your thoughts and send out, you will see again. Is it time, in your life yet to relinquish the "I can't" thinking? Put something more exciting in its place.

You are gonna' have to overcome fear for this replacement I am about to give. Just think like Braveheart, here is the antidote ..."I AM." Your words and thoughts are extremely contagious to each other. If the words you use are not creating the outcome you desire, eliminate their use from your vocabulary and replace them with words of creativity.

How would your life be today if you never learned to utter such words as "I can't," "It's impossible," or instead of telling God to build damns, you always, in your moments of frustration said, "God bless it!" Your words are the outer expression of your thoughts and set into motion precisely what you think.

Columbus, the great visionary, found us a wonderful place to live. We were able to escape from the English rule, thank God for that. If you are not sure what I'm talking about, rent the movies, "Braveheart" or "Rob Roy" and you'll get the picture. It was great that we escaped to the free land, good ol' USA, but what did we bring with us? Stay tuned for the answer. Here is a hint:

A group of scientists on a research program in the USA (you may read more about it in a book titled *People in Quandaries*), discovered as they were visiting an Indian reservation that the Indians did not stutter, not one full-blooded Indian in the country stuttered. Being most curious as to why not, they found there was no word, in all the Indian vocabularies that described the activity of stutter. Therefore, how could the Indians express an activity they had no written, verbal or mental reference for?

Now that is the hint for the answer, what did we bring with us to our land of freedom? Imprisonment, the slavery of the English vocabulary. Know the power in words and allow me to share some meanings of words, with you, for your enlightenment:

BAPTISM: The erasing power of the mind.

BELIEF: A state or habit of mind in which trust or confidence is placed in some person or thing. May suggest mental acceptance without directly implying certitude or certainty on the part of the believer.

CAREFUL: Marked by "painstaking" effort to avoid errors or omissions.

CHURCH: A public divine worship, body of believers, place people gather to unite in oneness.

CULT: Formal religious veneration; worship, a system of

religious believers and ritual.

DESIRE: Will, heart, to give birth to.

FATHER: Source, sun.

FEAR: Profound reverence and awe, especially toward God.

FORGIVE: Cancel out.

GUILT: Feeling of culpability for imagined offenses or from a sense of inadequacy. LORD, Law.

INTEGRITY: The quality or state of being complete or undivided. Openly exemplifying your true, heartfelt feelings in all circumstances, at all times, with all people, places, and things.

JUDGEMENT: From the Latin jus, – right, and dico, – I declare. It's a declaration of what is right or just (and is only in its secondary sense of what has been handed down to us acquired the meaning of "condemnation").

MEEK: Enduring injury with patience and without resentment, mild, focused, harnessed, guided power of love.

OCCULT: To hide from sight, not revealed, to cover up, secret, not easily apprehended or understood.

Kinda' reminds one of Jesus as He spoke in parable and ducked the crowd, when He made it too easy to understand His teachings, as they began to throw rocks. He spent a lot of time hiding from sight. Those people, as many still have today, had major fear. Jesus was, by definition, big time into the OCCULT, was he not?

PINEAL BODY: Seat of the soul.

PSYCHIC: Spiritual in origin, of the soul.

RELIGION: To unite (true meaning).

REPENT: To change one's mind.

SALVATION: Liberation from ignorance of illusion to be saved from the need of.

SHAME: A "painful" emotion caused by consciousness of guilt.

SIN: Original word "sine" when the archer missed the mark, or S̲elf I̲mposed N̲onsense will cover this one.

SORRY: Feeling sorrow, regret, energy waste and depletion or penitence, mournful, sad, inspiring sorrow, pity, scorn or ridicule, contemptible.

UNWORTHY: Lacking in excellence or value, poor, worthless base, dishonorable, undeserving

WORRY: Mental distress or agitation resulting from concern, anxiety, choke, strangle, torment, to harass by tearing, biting or snapping at the throat.

As you can see here, if you are not clear on what you are speaking, why keep speaking it? As for the description of careful, why go through life in your precious now moments in such pain. Instead of going around scared silly about everything that is out to get you, making statements like, "Oh, you gotta' be careful," how about making statements like, "You gotta' be clear, focused, balanced, and grounded."

Know that your words have instantaneous life changing power, 270 horsepower per word, AWESOME POWER. Kinda' makes you want to whisper instead of speaking the next time you get angry, huh? That would be a wise and an excellent choice.

Use words that build, not destroy. Make a deal with family or friends to awaken you to negative affirmations; unless, of course, your life reflects only health, wealth, prosperity, happiness, joy, success, peace, beauty, love, and harmony.

A change in your vocabulary will spark a change in your mind, which in turn will spark a change in your thoughts; which will result in different colors around you; which, if the new vocabulary is of an uplifting, positive nature, will cause a cure in you.

Pure words, pure thoughts, pure color, pure cure. That attitude cures Dis-ease.

CHAPTER 3

Color Cures Dis-Ease

I t is not unknown, in our day of higher consciousness, that certain colors trigger specific responses to the "emental" body; that is the emotional and mental part of us. Governments, law establishments, mental and medical institutions, corporations, and science know there are values, of degree, in the use of color to stimulate, activate or soothe the condition of the mind to invoke response or reaction toward certain mental stimulus.

You may view the color with your eyes or through the eye of the mind—third eye/pituitary gland—mental imagery according to the purpose or goal in your meditations and create cure in the area of your body or life with the color needed for the goal.

Please keep in mind, the power is YOU, not the color.

Red:

Energizes. Partially neutralizes x-ray and radiation damage. Assists in the relinquishing of limitations. Lethargy, inertia, depression, dead locks, ruts and inhibited sexual expression. Helps relieve congestion in the body, mind and emotions, the nervous system, blood, liver, circulatory and respiratory systems, colon, genitals, legs, overall physical body.

Magenta:

Aura builder, nourishes heart, kidneys, calms fear.

Scarlet:

Raises blood pressure, stimulates heart; caution, use with care. Don't wear it if you wish not to share it!

Orange:

Quiets digestion, soothes joints, decongests lungs. Assists in the releasing of repressed emotions and the attitude of resistance. The color of attraction, creativity, and joy of life can alleviate shyness or association with strangers or the opposite sex. Enhances harmony, sociability, creativity, and working together with others. It increases one's dominion over self, stimulates courage, authority, and assertiveness. Assists indigestion, circulation, and metabolism problems. Helps in pregnancy, helps lungs, colon, ovaries, spleen, pancreas, kidneys, bladder, and gallbladder.

Yellow:

Stimulates digestive organs, relieves worry, melancholy, benefits lymphatic system, blood, nerves, brain, skin, stomach, intestines, muscles, pancreas, liver, and gallbladder. Stimulates the ability to think more clearly. Transmutes sensual thoughts to a higher perspective with a li'l attention on the pituitary gland.

Lemon:

Detoxer, master cleanser, builds immune system.

Green:

Toner, builds muscles, reduces stomach acid. Promotes growth, peace, harmony, tranquility, benefits the nervous system, reduces stress, relieves fear associated with relationships. Regenerates cells, oxygenates blood vessels and heart. Benefits the reproductive system, thymus and pituitary glands, bones, and lungs.

Turquoise:

Smoothens skin, prevents scarring, builds hair and nails.

Blue:

Oxygenates the blood, lowers mid-range fevers. Gives poise, calm, and the inner feeling of power. The psychological, emotional, de-stress medicine. Helps growth, metabolism, vitality, thyroid, and parathyroid glands, throat, and nervous system.

Indigo:

Reabsorbs swellings, bruises, pain and tumors.

Violet:

Eases foul processes, bad breath, high fevers, shyness.

Purple:

Deep relaxer, lowers blood pressure, oxygenates cells.

ᴵndigo, Violet, Purple, and ᴵavender:

Are all similarly related to the manifesting power of YOU-SPIRIT and have qualities such as erasing, cleansing, relinquishing, stimulating, activating, and accelerating power. Invoke clairvoyance and transformation, benefit pineal, hypothalamus, and pituitary glands, blood, lungs, muscles, vision, hearing, and sense of smell. The shades from indigo to its lighter version, lavender, release hormones and a word that your science has yet to know the significance of, "razon," into the cellular systems of the body via the pineal and pituitary glands. The color assists in the purification and erasing of old, deep-seated mental blockages and negativities, to include emotional states. It helps to relax, exerts powerful healing influences, relieves neurosis, calms nerves, violence and irritability, purifies blood cells, helps control excessive hunger, promotes bone growth, brain transmittal, spleen, kidney, and bladder functions.

White:

Is and includes all colors and all shades, everything comes first from white. It assists in accelerating the vibration of anything you apply it to. The all-encompassing color of divine protection. Contemplate white light for 10–15 minutes a day to cure any dis-ease.

This book is not about how to cure the effects of disease, but how to prevent the effect by educating you on the cause.

Resistance to anything empowers the thing being resisted. You may have not contracted AIDS by resisting AIDS, but your resistance to your mother-in-law, or boss at work, or spouse, may have been the magnetizing effect. Whether the disease is AIDS, arthritis, diabetes, heart disorder or cancer. If YOU are the one it has come to, YOU are its magnet. YOU vibrated it to yourself.

We are generators of specific vibrations. If your attention is on a thing or activity you don't like or want, your resistance to this thing is negative vibrational current. This negativity will create for you some form of dis-ease to be with you (its creator) as long as you are in harmony with it.

Whatever you have in your life just now, you are in vibrational harmony with it.

Whatever you would like to have but don't have, you are not in vibrational harmony with it.

If something is in your life you don't want, you are in vibrational harmony with it. Your attention is what pulls you toward the vibration.

If you become aware of something you do not wish to have, "turn the other cheek," look away, focus on the thing you do prefer. Train yourself to shift your attention moment by moment away from anything dissatisfying.

Many teachers have come to us to teach the all-so-simple psychologies of the principles of universal law.

You will not make dis-ease, dis-cord or dis-harmony go away

by focusing on their effects. However, by knowing their cause, you now have opportunity for a more intelligent decision. There is great creating power and healing potential in deciding.

STOP resisting, start allowing to flow into the law of allowing.

STOP being bounced around like a pinball. Start deciding what you do want and flow into the law of deliberate creating.

STOP being a magnet for what you don't want by setting your attention on it, start flowing in the law of magnet attraction by focusing on what you do prefer. Hold the vision for a few minutes at a time through your day. Take five and hold the vision. Take five and hold the vision. Take five and hold the vision.

CHAPTER 4

Don't Color Me Red

Red represents a negative quality. True or false? Like black, the color red has been associated with negative qualities, so the answer is true. Red is also your willpower in color, so the answer is false. The answer is that red is neither a positive or negative color. It is just another color of the rainbow that represents the many different aspects of your emotional reflecting to life; your mind in color shaded by your response, reaction, or lack thereof. It is when black, brown, green, and other colors, attitudes, mix with red that show indications of less than good meanings, intentions or positive responses. Don't color me red! Why not? I'll tell ya' why not.

One morning, I was in the presence of a lady and her 13-year-old daughter. They were having a very long and heated altercation.

We were all headed to a metaphysical bookstore where there was an "aura" camera in operation.

The daughter had her picture taken first, under the influence of anger yes, but resistance, no. It came out a near transparent, bright scarlet red all the way around her, not even a hint of any other shade. Anger without remorse.

The mother very reluctantly, under the influence of the entire family, sat for her shoot. Her picture also came out all red, but quite a different shade. A thick, dull, fuzzy red may best describe it. Muddy red for anger, dull and fuzzy for resistance.

Both ladies took first place for the closest shades of scarlet and best exemplifying the attitude of "pissed off" that day.

I have discovered, after taking over 10,000 aura pictures, that most people are knowledgeable enough to know not to have their picture taken while under the influence of negativity.

The most common dark or muddy red auras I view are those of "The Human Teenager." God bless 'em as they go through the change; that is, from one potential mate to the next, the age-old role of Romeo dumping Juliet or vice versa. Even though the youthful adult has an idea that "it might not look good to see my aura now," Mom and Dad are standing by with some of that good ol' parental pressure, "Ah, come on! I'm buying." I often admonish the parent, but some do not mind if the kid goes through even more remorse by viewing those awful feelings and emotions in color.

The roles played that cause these muddy shades of red around you, as put forth in the *Celestine Prophecy* are intimidation, interrogation, poor me, and aloof. These attitudes come in some pretty muddy, dark, and ugly shades of red or scarlet. Now you know why Rhett Butler left. Quite frankly, he didn't "give a damn" for Scarlet.

Keeping in mind that all the different shades and combinations thereof, represent different attitudes, characters, personalities, and activities of the mind.

I was taking pictures for a group of about 35 one evening in Kansas City, Kansas. I was having a workshop with, for the most part, spiritually-minded people. I was halfway through a long line of people, snapping aura photos of each—then came the unique aura of the night.

A young man, maybe thirtyish, had bright red all the way around him. As he viewed his colors he was, let's say, unsatisfied. You see, he had aura photos of himself on other occasions and they were always white, gold, purple, blue and lavender, the more spiritual color vibrations of a higher note. As a matter of fact, this fella' came back after I had completed everyone else's pictures and he was a downright unhappy camper. I had previously given him a brief, but in this case unsatisfactory, explanation of the aura.

He said, "I am not red!"

I could sense a tone of seriousness in his voice. Then I quickly asked him, "Do you meditate?"

"A lot!" he exclaimed.

I asked, "Know you the term "kundalini"?

"Sure," he said. "That is what I have been meditating on for several months."

I asked, "Know where kundalini resides in the human body?"

"At the root chakra, bottom of the spine," he replied.

I asked, "Know the color there?"

He said, "It's Red!" as it dawned on him of his success in the bright red color all around him. "I've raised my kundalini energy!" He was so excited that he went around to all his friends showing off his beautiful, red spiritual aura.

Yes color, kinda' like humans, just because some display less than desired attitudes, doesn't mean the whole race is undesirable. If you feel the whole human race is undesirable, I would suggest you "Phone Home." We are just visitors here on earth. Meditate on your stellar home.

On another note: At another time I took a picture of a lady around 40. I had never seen a bright red heart chakra area like she had. This lady was not overweight and she carried her body quite well. I looked at her with empathy in my eyes and said, "Your heart is working too hard."

With a countenance of total shock, she said, "WHAT DID YOU SAY?"

I gently paraphrased, "Your heart is pumping too fast."

"OH MY GOD," she replied, "I was in for a physical this morning and my doctor said my heart was beating 20 beats a minute too fast.'

I admonished her, "If you don't believe your doctor and/or your aura, I recommend you go into the silence of where the blood of your body is being pumped and get your answer there."

She adjusted her schedule when she found out that I gave workshops in that bookstore. The next Tuesday she showed up. I brought the camera with me to view everyone's auras. This lady's aura, along with her visage, went from cardiac runner-up to a smooth shade of calm blue.

I asked, "What'd ya' do?"

As a huge smile blessed everyone listening, she said, "I'm a Realtor, I had 120 listings last week, but now I have 60!"

I said, "That's wonderful. Know the term "vacation?""

She said, "Not for years, but I soon will.""

I hope my book crosses the hands of this sweet lady so I can hear from her on how many more homes she sells now. I believe she was with Carol Jones Realty in Springfield, Missouri.

While taking pictures in Springfield, I took a mother/daughter set, mother first. She was red, orange, green, yellow, somewhat normal or average colors except the yellow was cloudy and covered her face with obvious worry or mental concern. We soon discovered why; it was her daughter's turn.

I'd say she was in her late teens and tense. I gave her gentle, soothing instructions to relax her tensions and stress before snapping her photo. To no avail. I could see after two minutes that her mind was not letting her body go anywhere related to my instructions of a peaceful place in her heart, or any similar state.

The proof soon followed as I peeled off the back of the film, only to view what I imagined, muddy dark red, left side and both shoulders. As her mother viewed with us, I—risking the possibility of the mother, feeling her dominance, being the thief—said, "Who has been stealing your energy?"

As she looked up at me with eyes of amazement, tears filling them promptly, her mother on override said, "I told you to get rid of him! He's nothin' but trouble!"

At this point I could see that it was not only the boyfriend causing the young lady's muddy red. Unconditional love was a subject we did not delve into at the time. I would normally provide 10 minutes with each person, not 10 months, which in psychological terms seemed to me what would be required to get started with this particular team.

I hope this reaches them too. However, it requires an ear to hear and the mind must be on "open" to receive truth.

I was at a bookstore in Sedona, Arizona taking pictures. A group of four or five stepped up. The first and most curious, a lady of fortyish. I peeled off the back of the photo for viewing, without yet showing her the picture, as we were all having fun laughing and carrying on. I looked at her and said, "You already know the problem, are you sure you wish to view it in color?"

As she began to bring her jaw, that had just hit the floor, back to her head, looking me squarely in the eyes, her friends pausing instantly in a moment of intense silence that came over the room, she said, "Let's see!" As she viewed the muddy red on her shoulders and all over her left side, she said, "What does that mean?"

I said, "Oh, easy question," as I pressed down on her shoulder firmly for about five seconds. I asked, "How's that feel?"

She replied, "Heavy."

I lifted my hand off, "And that?"

She said, "Relief."

Then I said, "Dump him!"

That stirred up the gang. They all started asking questions of her like, "How'd he know?" "Have you talked with him before?" I then explained the meaning of muddy red and how it usually reflects a muddy relationship of one sort or another.

They all not only had their pictures taken, but left the store, found some other people and brought them over too!

I did finish explaining to the lady with the muddy red around her, what I meant by "dump him." That, in brief, was to "dump the attitude of being a people-pleaser, the need-to-be-right attitude, or control of others."

Adopting unconditional understanding towards all the universe will bring you together with the ones who grow with you or release you from the ones who are no longer necessary in your soul's unfoldment. The universe just goes along for the ride. As you implement a change in the mind, the universe creates the circumstances and opportunities for your new desires.

This lady, bless her, gave me a hundred-dollar-bill as gratuity. With my hand still open, I said, "Oh, my dear, I do very well here in this field."

She interrupted me, as she closed my hand, saying, "You are why I came to Sedona." Meaning, of course, through the colors that represent her, I was able to define the problem and then reveal a solution for it. Receiving up to this point was still a characteristic I preached better than practiced.

The color red in itself is not a negative color. It emanates from the area at the bottom of your spine or root chakra, representing your energy for earth life and willpower. It sustains your body out on third dimension reality and helps bring to you your material manifestations.

When you give way to hostility, controlling of others, manipulation, abuse and the like, your original pure, raw, red energy darkens and becomes scarlet, maroon, and muddy murky shades. It poisons the aura or mind-body, and physical body as well. Other concepts, notions, activities, and perceptions of the mind that muddy up the aura are fear, judgment, shame, guilt, worry, hurry, and all their relatives and subsidiaries.

Imagine, at the death of the body—one day it will happen, right? You wake up, and in your new ultimate level of awareness... there He is on His throne. Big Daddy himself! Naturally you introduce yourself, "I'm..."

"Yes, I know."

"Now look Dad, let me explain. Oh, how much time do I have?"

"You wouldn't believe me if I told you, so go on."

"Okay, now it's like this here, see, I done went and got all saved, repented, forgiven, baptized, and absolutely accepted your boy as my personal guru lots of times, so what's happenin'?, you know?, like what now?"

"Well son, it's like this, do you recall my boy saying, 'Cast down your possessions?' "

"Yeah!"

"Well, why on earth did you remain in that lowly depressive state of fear? I mean, don't you remember the gentle nudges? I was trying to have fun through you, but no-o-o-o, you had to keep hanging onto fear rather than faith. You kept letting those control freaks buffalo you with that ridiculous idea of religion. I didn't say, 'Be religious.' As a matter of fact, I sent my boy to release that controlling attitude of all those dudes who wanted to control the planet I created for all of us to learn unity and to love all, experience growth, abundance and life, not to mention, party."

"Party?"

"Yes, I love ballroom dancing! Now, that's what I call having life more abundantly! But how could I enjoy through you, when you're puttin' that other God thing in front of me; you know, those possessions, fear, and the like?"

"Well, let me explain."

"Oh, you'll get your chance to explain all right and the next time you tell me to get a life, why don't you dump those possessions, so I can get one through you?"

"You remembered that?"

"Yep! Now it looks like you and me been talkin' long enough. Let me look at my earth watch. Yep, just as I thought, twenty earth years have passed and as you know, time is collapsing out there. So know ye the term, 'vacation away from home?' "

"Are you talkin' reincarnation?"

"That's an accurate term for it."

"Oh, but I don't believe in that."

"Precisely, that's why you're still doing it."

"But they told me you only live once and it's in your bible."

"Yes 'they' did, and it's not my Bible. Until you get the gist of the meaning of eternity, you will continue to think in such limiting ways. It will be most helpful for you to get your verbs in order."

"What do you mean?"

"In 'their' bible about this subject, in Hebrews 9:27, it states quite clearly, 'It is appointed unto men once to <u>die</u>. Not <u>live</u>.' A more proper translation would be, let go of ego."

"But how do you stop reincarnating out there?"

"When you believe that's the process of experiential evolution,

nigh shall be your ascension. Now try and get it right this time, will ya'?

"Rule #1   Have No rules."

"Rule #2   See Rule #1

"Be independent of the opinions of others, don't be a SNIOP

"That's:

> **S**usceptible to the
> **N**egative
> **I**nfluence of
> **O**ther
> **P**eople

"Make what others think of you none of your business. Live not by the leadership of leaders; be it institution, religion or education, but rather live by my messages to you—your feeling center. The kingdom you seek is within. Set your barometer on the exemplifying of JOY. Accoona matata, no worries, have fun!"

Red in its pure form, is simply your energy in color. It is how you apply it that shades it. Each and every different attitude has its own shade.

A pure, puffy, bright, vivid red may indicate a material goal or quest, strong desire, major change or even transmutation.

Pure red may represent willpower, passion, strength, endurance, assertion, determination, self-confidence, vitality, health, and/or the ability to work long hours.

Another thing about red is its opposite polarity, green. You know, the color of dollar bills! If you have plenty of red, that's energy used wisely; you may apply it toward the answer to all material things—yes, greenback.

May you live long and prosper!

Remember Who You Are

CHAPTER 5

Creating With Orange

On a creative day, you will emit plenty of bright orange. On a very busy creative day, there will be plenty of red surrounding the orange; the orange representing the way in which energy is being expressed.

If you have just recently moved, are in the process of moving or are planning to move soon, most of your orange will be on the left side of your body, representing the change or upcoming change in your material status. The further away from the body the orange is on the left side, the more distant the material activity. Orange on your left side may also represent change in career, job or vocation of any sort. This could be the employing of someone or, if you are the boss, the releasing of an employee. If you are the employee, you could be gaining or losing a boss or co-worker. More often than any other meaning, orange on the left will represent change with career.

A full bright orange around you indicates excitement or joy of life. Someone living life to the fullest, enjoying the process as it happens in the moments of the now, exemplifying affluence, the garnishing of abundance, fulfillment of career, and/or domestic life.

Persons applying artistic abilities, inventing or creating, will have yellow close to the head with orange surrounding the yellow. The more focused on or enjoyment of the activity, the brighter the shades and more pure.

This would be the basic color orange. However with a brown mixture, life in general is muddy, often representing selfish attitudes. Like the character of the shrink played by Richard Dreyfuss in the movie, "What About Bob?"

Now, if you will think about yellow for a few moments, you will begin to emit yellow, not because you are visualizing yellow but because you are thinking.

CHAPTER 6

ᛒhe ᛒhought of Yellow

Yellow and gold manifest from the center of your being or as has been called, the Lord God of your being at the area of the solar plexus.

The color is gold and/or yellow and represents your thoughts, intellect, intuition, and communication. Although all communication is stimulated from this area of the body, it quickly goes through many areas of the body and normally ends up where you *think* you should think from. Yes... the head where so many, if not most, human thoughts are given to final consummation. Therefore, creating the mental atmospheric conditions we all enjoy living in today.

"How sad," I could say here, but of course, I won't.

That would just be another sad thought added to the already bulging pool of lack, want, and limitation many are now experiencing, right?

When one is mentally active thinking of a specific goal, the more clearly one sees the vision or outcome of said goal, the more clear the yellow around the head will be. This is where the yellow will be drawn. The more material-based the goal, the more orange, for the mundane, will mix with the yellow.

One day I was in the garage, being my li'l creative self, inventing some apparatus with metals and wood, for a new career I was entering. I was using different power tools, the need to be careful was with me, as was the need to be original in my creation.

After completion of my projects in the garage, I went in that evening, watched some "how-to" videos, and read some manuals. With all this new information plus the project I was working on earlier in the garage now assembled, I asked a friend to take a picture of me with the new aura imaging photography system I had just set up. Because electromagnetic computers and high tech are not among my "normal" things to do, I was sure I had "thought a record-breaker" in thinking when I put it together.

So let's see how my aura looked in the midst of it all. The shades were all very clear and bright; red, for the heavy workload of the day and passion; orange above me, just below the red for creative material endeavor, earth life stuff; and yellow, the clear thoughts of, "This is going together TONIGHT!"

It runs in the family DNA I suppose. There is but one time to have my cake and when it arrives, I don't sit around wondering when to eat it, I'm a man! Good thing my mama is a woman, men don't like waiting nine months for nuttin'. Green, on my right side, as I face the camera, bright and so clear. The energies passing through me were creative and I was certain that I would make this contraption work TONIGHT! Orange, on my left side (ring finger side) represents new career and near future move, which both took place over the next two months.

Now let's take a look at a different shade of yellow, one with a hazy, fuzzy tint of orange. The young lady I took this picture of was living in one of the most common states in the United States at the time. The state of Worry. The muddy yellow covered her face so you could just barely see only the eyes. Of course, in her opinion, she had plenty of justification for visiting that particular state. She was moving across the country with a ten-year-old-boy, a thirteen-year-old-daughter who was "NOT going with her and I mean NOT!!!," a cat that hated auto rides, and the wildest of all living mammal species, A Basenji (small doggie). The original meaning for the word Basenji is "beast." Did I mention unknown career lies ahead, unsold house stays behind? There is more here to add, plenty more, but you probably have the picture by now. Just like my mama used to always say, "Worry does what worry is," or was that Forest Gump?

In this case, if you look up the word worry in the dictionary, you will understand why I proceed *does* with *is*. Worry distorts any desires or goals you coulda' had in focus, causing destruction to the potential outcome of that segment of your lived time and space. I wouldn't worry about it though, because fortunately there is a color that may assist in the healing of that condition, so now let's turn to greener pastures.

Remember Who You Are

CHAPTER 7

Healing With Green

A bright, clear emerald green around you represents attitudes of health, growth, healing, help, assistance, and peace. With peace of mind, all the above that are higher vibrations can reach the intended or needed destinations of the body, mind, and soul pathing an avenue for the regenerated electrons to restore and uplift the cellular structure that you are. "Be still and know that the 'I AM' of you may be reached in peace, but not in chaos, electromagnetic discumbobulation, or stressed-out perception."

When blue comes in with its calming power and mixes with green, causing teal, you have the color that can heal the body, mind, and soul—kind of a package deal, huh?

More seriously, it takes all three; body, mind, and soul, in good condition to experience a life of enjoyment. The most beautiful teal I have ever witnessed was around a most beautiful soul; for book reference, I will call her amazing Grace because that is her name. Her greens and blues, making teal, are a reflection of her intent to help, assist, and heal others. I suppose you might say that's par for the course when you not only carry the title of Reiki Master, but exemplify it in every way. What a genuine sweetheart she is. A true blue devoted master healer.

With a large amount of forest green on your left side, something in the order of healing, growth, or assistance is headed your way. On the right side, a clear emerald green will indicate one who is creating with pure focus, knows where they are going and how to get there.

A bright luminous blue/green shows some of the highest of human qualities; deep empathic compassion and the vital force of perfect adaptability. I have experimented on people in the healing fields with my aura camera, snapping many before and after pictures of the healing works they performed. I've come to the awareness that blue and green are the colors that represent the effect of/or intent to heal, help, or assist.

Reading between the lines of the more common meanings, I snapped a shot of a fella' one day while I was working a bookstore.

As I peeled off the back, I noted a bright white and teal beaming out of each ear. After I viewed it, I assimilated in my mind, that he had a unique experience, to say the least. I said, "Been doing some astral travel, huh?"

The fella's eyes enlarged as he grabbed for the photo saying, "Let me see that! How can you tell that? I went on an astral journey this morning, but how can you tell?"

Although I guessed at it, it was easy enough to answer his question. Many who experiment with astral travel use sound, and the streaks of light were from the ears.

May you go in green's peace.

ᴐrue ᗷlue

While taking pictures of eartheans at a bookstore in Spring-field, Missouri, a couple in their age of wisdom stepped up to my area and were very ready to see a shot of their auras. Well, I was very careful with this li'l' ol' gal, as I assisted her gently into the chair for her photo. All the while hoping this old couple's auras wouldn't scare off all the potential clients standing around.

There must have been over fifteen others waiting to see what was going on at this part of the store. Before they would become brave enough to see their own aura, they awaited the outcome of the couple I was working with. In my old-fashioned judgment, I ass...u...me...d that this couple, slow as they got around, had some pretty worn out old auras. Well, you know what they say about judging a book by its cover. Now here comes the time to peel off the back of their pictures. I took the lady first, of course. As I opened her photo, my judgment reached out to touch someone, right in the center of my heart, with an awestruck expression I'm sure was on my face. I was not expecting an aura I would want to advertise to the crowd. Low and behold, the beauty of a bright, pure, aqua-blue midday sky all around this woman. This woman's aura was so radiant! I knew at that moment I was in the presence of a magnificent soul, if not an ascended master. I literally had a shift in consciousness. Big lesson for this guy on how to judge humans—don't! Now I just figure that no matter what their physical appearance, they are God, or at least a close facsimile of that image.

As I held both of their pictures in my hands, his very close in the blue shade as hers, and plenty of it, I held them up to face the crowd and said, "This lady and her gentleman have the color of loyalty, honesty, devotion, truth, serenity, and calm. Now let's verify the devotion part."

I looked to the lady and asked, "How long have y'all been married?"

She proudly replied, "FIFTY ONE YEARS!"

After watching how affectionate the gentlemen was toward his wife, it was no wonder why they had such pure, powder blue auras of calm serenity. He treated her with uncommon respect.

One evening a nurse was relaxing on the couch, lovin' up her new babies; a small kitty and puppy, either one would give you a bath, they were most lovable. This lady, like so many people in the medical field, had blues and greens in her aura. The only exception, this evening, was how smooth and pure the bright greenish-blue was and her right side was lit up as if on fire with a bright luminous pinkgenta (that's magenta with pink in it) showing the affection toward the pets.

One time I was working a fair with my camera and had the opportunity to spend 30 minutes doing deep breathing exercises before performing a healing on a small child named Courtney who lived her life in a wheelchair. Before the fair opened and before I met li'l Courtney, I came from the breathing exercises and sat in the chair for a photo to see what color the intent to heal, coupled with Rosicrucian breathing techniques would look like in the aura. I had become a powder puff, sky blue, very bright light and very pure all around my head and shoulders.

After talking with Courtney's mother awhile, I performed the healing or transferred the energy to the li'l one. Not that she couldn't get out of the wheelchair, but she did not get back in it for at least an hour. She was one happy camper after that, plus of course, taking her picture and her little brother's picture brightened her face. I believe she had Cerebral Palsy. I never asked, but at least for a time, it didn't seem to get in her way of having fun.

Oh yeah, someone in the medical field may question my treating a patient without knowing what they had; like they know what each of their patients have before treatment. Not to mention the medicine I use has no title, known origin, or price and it doesn't even belong to me. All I do is call upon it, allow it to flow through me and say thank you.

May blue be with you.

Remember Who You Are

CHAPTER 9

Purple Power

Purple, violet, indigo, lavender, all somewhat different shades, with basic similarity. This variation of colors emanate from the brow of your head area and are, for simple terms, your connecting link with the spiritual power within you.

Leonardo da Vinci stated, "Use violet in your visualizations and it will increase the power of your meditations by ten times." This quote is paraphrased.

I am not familiar with any reference of Jesus applying this color in his meditations. I assume he was quite aware of the power in color vibration as well as affirmation, thought, aroma therapy, crystals, and most, if not all the external tools at our disposal for magnifying certain moods or settings of atunement for atonement (at-one-ment).

With rare exception, when I see what I call lollipop purple around the throat area, which is the area or chakra of personal power, mediation, and inner travel, it represents one who is very conscious of astral or soul travel and/or at least very vivid dream activity. I've had enough feedback on this to be convinced of its activity in color. What I am finding unusual is that more and more it is the young humans, mostly female, with this lollipop purple at the throat. What I find interesting here is that I understand children, since the early 1990's, are coming unto earth connected on a blue or purple ray and of course, we are graduating in awareness.

The tide of masculine is merging or balancing its polarity, "thank God," and feminine or Aquarian Age (golden age) is gradually assuming its full position within us cellularly, as well as celestially. This is not precognition or hearsay. We have been in this vibration for some years now and are becoming more aware of it—that's all.

The color violet is held at the brow or face area, brow chakra. Through it emerges spirit, who you are, or your spiritual power. The use or visualization of violet in your meditations assists greatly in the purging of fear, all gone bye-bye. You may call on St. Germaine to assist here and he will.

As I worked the stores in Sedona, Arizona, I often met people who see auras very well. I suppose you have already assumed how the subject would arise, as the field I am in would provide for such an initiation of the topic with nearly any stranger. During the period I was deeply involved in invoking the violet flame. I was including ascended master St. Germaine, asking to be immersed in it. People began to mention that I had violet or purple around me. There is an affirmation that will help you connect with the power in this color, kinda' bonds you together: "I AM THE RESURRECTION OF THE VIOLET FLAME."

Violet also assists in the purification process of white blood cells, a form of baptism, you might say. Violet carries with it the highest nature of vibrations. It has been called "MESSENGER OF THE GODS."

May the violet flame be with you.

Remember Who You Are

CHAPTER 10

The Truth
In White

From white comes all colors, all vibrations, and from it is dispensed all nature of activity. The color of protection, cleansing and ultimate baptism, erasing power of the mind.

If you are ever using colors for chakra opening/balancing, auric grounding, healings, zen, zar, transcendental meditations or yoga and are undecided on which color to apply, just use white. It will know what to do from there.

You may feel white's awesome power by simply closing your eyes at this very moment in your life. Go ahead, you have been given permission. Life will pause, at least yours will, as you pause it. Take a deep breath and release all tensions. Visualize white of the brightest, purest nature entering at the top of your head, growing down your spine out of your solar plexus, enveloping your entire body. Bask in the radiance of the color of the light bearer as you become.

One morning I hugged an angel.

As I was taking aura pictures in Sedona, a most wonderful lady approached the camera with her girlfriend and asked if I would take her picture. After shooting, I opened it, WOW! Never had I seen so much white around a human and the white was surrounded with a pink border. Normally I wait until I have completed the short reading of the client's photo before hugging the human good-bye. However, after viewing this unmistakable color combination of divine love, I made an exception. As I looked at her and said, "You're an angel," reaching out my arms, "and they hug!" What a hug! I was expecting special, but not like what I received. This was definitely not your average kinda' hug. From this being I embraced radiant love, compassion, warmth and tranquillity all in one hug. Memories like "Flash Dance" and "What A Feeling" came to mind.

In through the front door of the store walked a paradox about then. My angel lady looked across the room where the thunder emerged and gently shouted, "Hon, we're over here."

"Hon" was a seven-foot cowboy, weighing in at about 340 pounds; along with him, his six-and-half-foot partner. It was early afternoon and most obviously these ol' boys had been hittin' the till already; which led me in my judgment to wonder, "What's a small, beautiful blond, with the magnanimous heart of an angel, doing with a guy like this?

After I took the their pictures and went into conversation with them, I discovered her hubby to be a gentle-as-a-lamb human being. I certainly had my meditations for that evening cut in stone. Judgment and perception-clearing was their content. As the foursome departed, I received a hug from each of them.

The angel lady returned with a copy of her photo and as I promised her, I've displayed it ever since.

White is the activity of creation at work, the color of the most high vibration.

Christ is God in action; pure love, pure perfection, pure bliss, pure white.

Remember Who You Are

CHAPTER 11

Colors in Brief

The first seven colors are not only the basic colors of our rainbow, but also of, and related to, our energy inlet/outlet system called chakras. Beginning with the first or root chakra which is red, and going up the spine to the seventh chakra which is violet to white. Then we will give the meanings in brief of several of the less basic earth colors.

NOTE:

When you learn about the aura, you can begin to see and appreciate the profound and unique splendor of your own energy.

REMEMBER: Every color has its unique qualities and purposes. Imagine a color wheel. Each color is a location on the wheel. No color is better than another. Each has its inherent lessons, and challenging traits.

The right side: indicates one's expressive, active, or masculine side, the personality one projects outward, how other people see us.

The left side: indicates one's feminine, receptive or feeling side, the part of the personality that receives, feels, accepts, and imagines. The color in this position is also indicative of what one is creating for him/herself in the near future. If there is an abundance of color here, the person may be focusing most of their attention in the future. If there is a lack of color here, the person may be dwelling on past memories and events.

The center and above the person's head: indicates what the person is experiencing in the present moment. If there is a band of color stretching like an arc over the top of the person, this indicates what the hopes, goals, and aspirations are. For example, an indigo blue arc may indicate the person's highest aspirations may be spiritual or artistic. A red arc would indicate more physical, monetary or business goals.

Auras that expand out: indicate high energy, expressiveness, extroversion, social activity, desire for connection, gregariousness, positive outlook, sense of adventure, *or an expanded aura could indicate spiritual expansion.*

Auras closer in: indicate inward focus, sensitivity, desire for solitude, meditation, peace, tranquillity, or rest. *This could mean a need to express or move out.*

Red

Willpower, energy, vitality, courage, self-confidence.

POSITIVE OR NEUTRAL

BRIGHT:
Excitement, activity, passion, boldness, motivation, emotional enthusiasm, new birth, creative force.

CLEAR:
Concentration, active focus.

LIGHT:
Joyful experience, sensitivity, femininity.

DEEP:
Eroticism, stimulation, sensuality, desire.

PURE ROSE:
Unselfish affection, awakening of latent abilities.

NEGATIVE

BRIGHT BRICK RED:
Hostility, rage, overstimulation, impulsiveness, hate, intimidation, resent, force of will.

REDDISH BROWN:
Selfishness, guilt, fear.

ROSE BROWN:
Selfish affection, "let me obligate you," possessiveness.

BLACKISH RED:
Altercations, wrath, malice, avarice.

DULL:
Greed, resistance, "want to be right" syndrome.

Orange

**Joy of life, creativity, change,
love of adventure and excitement.**

POSITIVE/NEUTRAL

NEGATIVE

BRIGHT:
Attraction, major change, emotional, sociability.

CLOUDY:
Agitation, worry, lack purpose, confusion.

DEEP-PURE:
Success, sensation, authority, strength, artistic, warmth.

MUDDY:
Emotional imbalance, flamboyance, vanity.

BRIGHT ORANGE-YELLOW:
Sharp intellect, self confidence, industriousness, inventive, communication, intuition, exhilaration, spontaneity, openness

ORANGE-BRICK RED:
Low type of cunning, intolerance, aloof, snobbish.

Yellow

Communication, Intellect, Intuition.

POSITIVE OR NEUTRAL

BRIGHT:
Faith, self discipline, talented, optimism.

PURE:
Spiritual communication, sensitivity.

CLEAR-BRIGHT:
Understanding, wisdom, illumination, clairvoyance, clairsentience, openness.

NEGATIVE

CLOUDY WITH A TINT OF GREEN:
Excessive thought, worry, analytically critical, desire of recognition, dogmatic, bitter, egotism, indecision.

Green

Growth, healing, help, assistance, peace

POSITIVE/NEUTRAL

BRIGHT:
Abundance, prosperity, fertility, expansion, hope, regeneration.

LIGHT CLEAR:
Adaptability, empathy, the magic color used by fairies.

PURE:
Emotional stability, harmony, well being, acceptance, compassion.

BLUE/GREEN (Teal):
Ability to heal, contentment.

DARK OR DEEP
(Forest Green):
Self expressiveness, tolerance, rest.

SEA GREEN:
Emotional healing.

NEGATIVE

YELLOW/GREEN:
Jealousy.

GRAY/GREEN:
Deceit, cunning.

REDDISH/BROWN, GREEN:
Possessiveness.

CLOUDY YELLOW/ GREEN:
Indecisive, confusion, doubt, uncertainty, depression, heartbreak, imbalance

CLOUDY BROWNISH/ GREEN:
Selfishness, infidelity, fraud, subterfuge, clandestine.

Blue

Meditative, inner travel, calm, loyalty.

POSITIVE/NEUTRAL

DEEP/DARK:
Inner peace, religious feeling, honesty, serenity, patience, reserve, reverence, reliability, good judgment, forgiveness, the will to do God's work, power of the spoken word.

BRIGHT:
Devotion, truth, harmony, understanding, creative, self expression, gentleness

LIGHT:
Solitude, active imagination.

CLEAR:
High degree of spirituality, tranquility, clairaudience.

LIGHT/BRIGHT: (Teal)
Active healing, power to heal emotionally, physiologically, and psychologically.

BLUE/LAVENDER:
High idealism.

NEGATIVE

CLOUDY:
Blocked perception, melancholy, apathy, forgetfulness, over sensitivity.

REDDISH/BROWN/BLUE:
Selfish religious feeling.

GRAY/BLUE:
Religious feelings of fear.

BLACKISH/BLUE:
Religious superstition.

DARK/CLOUDY:
Fear, depression, worry.

REDDISH/BLUE/CLOUDY:
Domineering

LAVENDER PALE GRAY:
Fear

Indigo

Spiritual power, protection, meditation power,
psychic development, wisdom, faith, imagination.

POSITIVE/NEUTRAL

*BRIGHT VIOLET
TO LAVENDER:*
Forgiveness, dignity, spiritual
dedication, kindness, magic,
mysticism, profundity, supernatural abilities, artistic intuition, divine creativity, human
love, independence, transformation, healing power.

LAVENDER:
Releasing of hormones, razon
monadic essence, holy spirit,
prana, chi, Christ consciousness into the cellular system of
the body.

LOLLIPOP PURPLE
(at throat area):
Important intuitive dreams,
soul or astral travel.

NEGATIVE

*CLOUDY OR MIXED WITH
BLACK, RED, OR BROWN:*
Intense erotic imagination,
overbearing, "poor me" syndrome, vying for sympathy,
feelings of separateness or
being misunderstood, irritable,
seriousness, caution, skepticism, materialism, pursuit of
profit.

White

Color of the light bearer or light worker. Truth, unity, aspiration, inspiration cosmic awareness, motivation.

POSITIVE/NEUTRAL

BRIGHT:
Protection, purity, perfection, awakening of great creativity. Dissolver of limitations and barriers or blockages.

BRIGHT/PURE:
Deep meditation, conscious contact or communication with source. Inspiration, cleansing of self ego, enlightenment, Christ consciousness.

MOTHER OF PEARL WHITE:
Power to resurrect.

CRYSTAL WHITE:
Power of ascension.

NEGATIVE

DULL-CLOUDY:
Day dreaming, energy buildup, physical pain, lack emotional balance. Holding back from expressing self.

Shades between the basic colors of the seven basic chakras. To include White's opposite polarity, Black:

Black

Absorption, balancing, grounding.

POSITIVE/NEUTRAL

PURE/CLEAR:
Secretive, the unknown, latent
ability, subconscious protection, destruction of negative
energy, shield of protection.

NEGATIVE

*MUDDY MIXTURE WITH
ANY COLOR:*
Fear, denial, guilt, shame, lack,
burdens, abuse, imbalance,
absence of light, hidden truth
unrevealed.

Brown

New growth, industry.

POSITIVE/NEUTRAL

PURE:
Establishing of new roots,
desire to accomplish, organization.

NEGATIVE

CLOUDY:
Selfishness, jealousy,
conditionalism, unloving
towards self, hatred, materiality. Need for cleansing. Clog-
ging energies at the chakras.

RED/BROWN:
Possessiveness.

*BROWN MIXING WITH
GREEN, RED OR YELLOW:*
Charlatan, subterfuge, clandes-
tine, cheating.

GRAY/BROWN:
Depression, discouragement.

Burgundy

Sensually active mind, sexual activity, deep emotional affection.

POSITIVE/NEUTRAL

NEGATIVE

BRIGHT:
"Turned on," in the mood for romance.

Overactive sex-life (I put this on the negative side to balance out the page. Sex is not of a negative quality. The cosmic law is that you be conceived through copulation.

xcuse me, as I interrupt this book, to bring you a special insight, so as to familiarize you with this shade of the basic reds. One afternoon, I took a picture of a thirteen-year-old. I peeled off the back to view the photo and to my surprise, saw BRIGHT, PURE BURGUNDY all over her left side coming up over her left shoulder indicating this activity was with her in the present.

I reacted saying, "I THOUGHT YOU WERE JUST SEEING CHARLEY AS A FRIEND!"

To my reaction she responded, "Shhhh!"

Her mother was around the corner in the other room. She grabbed my arm and lead me into the kitchen and began to explain how "It just happened."

I interjected, "Well, young lady, excuse me, WOMAN, before your mama discovers you have been out sowing wild oats, you had better start praying for a crop failure before it "just happens" that you become a full-time babysitter! I mean besides white light I am hoping you used some form of a more material type of protection." She went on to explain how she was in touch with the cycles, which came to me as an enlightening shock.

I exclaimed, "I'm glad you are in touch because I think your mama's gonna' be touchin' you with that old wooden paddle she used for you kids when you where li'l farts."

You see, this teenager knew she'd been had when she viewed the bright burgundy; and being on her left shoulder, she knew it represented the NOW, and she knew that I was accurate at defining the color's meaning and placement.

As I soon discovered, it is not always the case that this shade of red indicates someone romancing a lover, at least not one with arms and legs. Let me share.

There I was, taking photos one morning, in a bookstore in Sedona. I snapped a shot of an attractive young lady with this same shade of burgundy on her left side rising up to her shoulder. I stood back with the smirk of great confidence on my mug and said, "New boy friend, huh?"

Thinking I had this one nailed down pretty well from my little, but profound experience of it, she said, "NOPE!"

Among us were a few others observing her reading and awaiting the next utterance from my lips. I said, "Girl friend."

She said, "Not even."

I said, "New pet, long lost relative, horse you love to ride, dolphin you've been petting."

She said, "No!, no!, no! and no!"

I became nervous. I breathed deep and smooth. I regained my composure and then firmly spoke, "This particular shade of red is indicative of the phenomenon commonly referred to as 'emotional turn-on.' It's governed by the root and/or navel chakra system of the human vehicle termed body. These areas and colors always represent the earthly, mortal, material, or mundane activities or notion thereof. There are no exceptions to this law of the human anatomy in color." I went on, as I began to lighten the explanation with my Elvis voice impression, "Now this bright, vivid red on your left means someone or something has turned you on, or Don Juan Demarko is about to walk through the door any moment because this color, being on your shoulder, represents this energy is working with you, like now!"

She smiled, looked teasingly into my eyes and said, "Would it have a bearing on it, that I purchased a new Corvette yesterday?"

At this point, I have to ask "yourself" just one question, are you kinda' gettin' the meaning of the meanings of this particular shade of red?

Gold

True, coming into one's own power, dynamic spiritual energy, great higher inspiration, activation of alchemical power, strong enthusiasm, revitalization, healing, harmony, attraction of abundance.

POSITIVE/NEUTRAL

RUBY/GOLD:
Stimulates one to minister unto others.

NEGATIVE

CLOUDY:
Still in the process of awakening.

Lavender

Carries the cleansing power of hormones/razon to and through the blood system (as in baptism), relinquishes limitations and fear, psychic purification, healing to the four lower bodies, dignity.

POSITIVE/NEUTRAL

PURE/CLEAR:
Awesome healing power.

NEGATIVE

CLOUDY:
Overbearing, intolerance, martyrism.

Magenta

Emotional "turn-on," magnetism, arousal, emotionally affectionate, love toward mother earth or animals.

POSITIVE/NEUTRAL

NEGATIVE

BRIGHT:
Sexual passion or excitement.

CLOUDY:
Over balanced sexually, manipulative, persuasive, conditional.

Pink

Divine affection, purest love, appreciation, empathy, compassion, selflessness, caring, soft, likable.

POSITIVE/NEUTRAL

NEGATIVE

PURE/CLEAR:
Highest order of human love.

CLOUDY:
Need for recognition.

Silver

Awakening of feminine energies, imagination, abilities of illumination, creative intuition.

POSITIVE/NEUTRAL

NEGATIVE

SPARKLING SILVER:
Fertility, pregnancy (during and up to nine months after), creativity is being activated within.

CLOUDY:
Physical imbalance, recluse, hermit, loner, secretive, obsessive, compulsive disorder.

Remember Who You Are

CHAPTER 12

Quick Color Reference

The most general meaning of these colors when they are bright, pure or clear:

AQUA .... Teacher, healer

AZURE .... Direct order of healing

BLACK .... Grounding

BLUE .... Calm

BROWN .... Industrious

BURGUNDY .... Sexual activity

CARMINE .... Human affection

CRIMSON .... Sensually stimulated or angry (*what can I say, some people are mad lovers*).

GOLD .... Spiritual abundance

GREEN .... Health, growth, healing

GRAY .... Unveiling innate creative abilities

INDIGO .... Spiritual power

IVORY .... Energy build up

LAVENDER .... Cleansing, purifying power

LILAC .... Altruism

MAGENTA .... Emotional affection

MAROON .... Sensual energy

MAUVE .... Feeling mentally limited

ORANGE .... Attraction, change, creativity

ORCHID........................... The illuminated clairvoyant

PEACH .... Gentle strength and joy

PINK................................. Affection

PURPLE .... Spiritual power

RED .... Energy

ROSE .... Self love, unselfish affection

RUBY .... Stimulates healing of emotions

SCARLET .... Self pride *(Rhett Butler's lover)*

SILVER............................. Illumination

SILVER SPARKLES .... Pregnancy

TEAL .... Physical or emotional healing

TURQUOISE .... Meditative awareness

VIOLET .... Spiritual power

WHITE .... Truth *(all colors come from white)*

YELLOW........................... Communication, Clairvoyance

CHAPTER 13

Spinning Wheels

$\mathcal{I}$n Sanskrit vocabulary, the word chakra /ˈshä-kra / means spinning wheel. For easy reference, we shall call your seven basic energy centers "chakras."

These writings are intended to stimulate one basic effect in you, that is, to get you mentally conditioned to open up to the universal powers already available to you. It is said that the entire universe resides within the human spine. Be absolutely certain that you no longer harbor the old-fashioned concept that if you have, get, acquire, or use too much of this universal supply, "there won't be enough for others." The source is infinite and always turned on.

Imagine Jesus saying to the multitude of five thousand: "Yep, we're fresh out of fish. Guess you dudes and dudettes are gonna' starve."

What this has to do with your chakra system is all about the psychology of your mind, your attitude, and your preconditioned mind set of lack, want, and limitation. This has greatly assisted in the shutting down of these vital centers, supposed to be flowing with the energies from spirit to soul to mind to body, so as to bring you to a heaven on earth kinda' life.

I understand there will soon be an opening of five more chakras in addition to the existing seven in the human body, that are fairly non-op in most humans. These energy centers affect the human DNA or your molecules. There is, by the way, a thirteenth—not in body. Let's say, above the rest in vibration. The significance of these twelve centers of inner activity may be better understood with much study. However, to get an idea of your relationship with your chakras (twelve), here are a few considerations to contemplate.

If you take thirteen balls of even size, it will take twelve to cover one so it is hidden. There were twelve disciples around Jesus. We have twelve calendar months. There are twelve signs of the zodiac enveloping our solar system. There were twelve special tribes. There are twelve basic playing cards, four suits. These originated for the soul purpose of giving direction to the Kings. They were in stone until the gypsies got a hold of 'em, condensed them, then used them for earning silver on their travels. There are twelve cranial nerves that surround the pineal body. These interact with the chakras, senses, and entire endocrine system. Some say we have twelve basic dimensions. Twelve is a vibration in relationship with the human body and the energy system that stimulates it through the chakras.

There are many books written on what caused our disconnection with these other five chakras and why the basic seven we still have, are mostly inoperable. What's most important here is accelerating the vibration of those you now have that are activatable. Giving conscious attention to the seven will stimulate the other inert pow-ers we have accessible as our personal evolution allows:

lst: ROOT CHAKRA. The color is red. The sound is DOE in C. Location, pubic region, base of spine. This primal material force is your energy and willpower. This is a powerful chakra because it is the home of Kundalini (awesome life force).

The love vibration is raising on our planet and consequently many are experiencing the raising of Kundalini and most, unaware of what the heaven is going on. This spontaneous raising of the life force called Kundalini has increased so much that groups have been set up to assist. The standard medical field hasn't a clue. You could spend months in a hospital at $3,000 a day, for something they have no cure for. Or you can meditate, ground, and balance yourself for no charge. For heaven's sake, DO NOT allow the practice of someone trained in the dark ages, to pump dye into your spinal column or cut into it.

I recommend, just in the case you are a likely candidate for Kundalini raising, that you become accustomed to sitting up straight and doing your meditations this way. You could think of the root chakra as your ambassador to the third dimension. This area deals with your level of physical energy, fear and all of its relatives, subsid-iaries, and emotional areas. It is this color that emits in a fit of rage. Not to be confused with a bright red that may simply indicate high energy.

Personally I do not recommend meditating on the root or navel, especially root chakra, for more than a few seconds, and this for the purpose of balancing them with the higher chakras. These two are already open and supplying you with enough physical energy that they need not be emphasized. However, in the need of more energy from lack of courage, alertness, or lethargy, the root chakra is the one to accelerate.

2nd NAVEL CHAKRA, the color is orange. The sound is RAE in D; location, navel area. This energy center governs your reproductive, physical and emotional issues of creativity and sexuality, joy in life vitality, youth, physical growth, new ideas, and change.

Please note: This is the area and color of attraction. If you happen to be one of the many millions in the mind set of attracting Mr. or Ms. soulmate; yes, this is the energy zone through which that may be accomplished.

Please allow me to admonish you on a cosmic fact. The universal law of attraction will provide you with whatever you continually focus upon. How do you really know what you're gonna' get? If you dare to set your sights on a specific person, you may play hell getting rid of them when you discover that they happen to be a serial killer or fatal attraction of unexpected proportion.

Here is one of the universal secrets. You may take the guesswork out of it once you have become the kind, type, sort-of character, personality, or individual you desire. The persons you attract will be in nature as the way in which you act. Your safest, surest method of attracting your desire is to balance this area with the others and make your decisions from the largest chakra center, the heart.

There is much in this book on how to become your own best friend and therefore, attract the same. There are many others. Read them to get an understanding on the subject if it is pressing on you. Resolve this all-so-common mystery by spending your thoughts on being the loving soulmate you idealize to all you meet. Your own self-realization will produce in your consciousness, what you feel is missing. If this means materially, Mr. or Ms. right for you will appear. I highly recommend that you search only within, it's all there, NOT AT THE BAR!

When a half circle attracts a half circle it does not make a whole circle. Not anymore than when a two-legged dog walks beside another two-legged dog does it make a four-legged dog. They still have the same amount of legs when they entered the relationship; as you are the same character, no matter how long you fake it. But do remember what Cary Grant said about faking it. If you continue you will make it. Not to be confused, remain in your integrity on the way. I mean, do you really want to be the one you are acting like?

When you feel a lack of courage, meditate on this area, imagining orange along with the attitude you would need breaking a new-to-you horse, or meeting a not-so-nice dog on a strange farm.

3rd SOLAR PLEXUS CHAKRA, the color is yellow. The sound is ME in E; location, solar plexus. The chakra center that governs our intuition, intellect and communication. This area, being unbalanced, allows one to fall prey to the fear of lack, want, and limitation. It may cause one, by these feelings, to assert control over others. Simply facing these feelings head-on, and asking them what they are there to teach you, will immediately relinquish any negative reactions. The miracle here is the willingness to experience your emotions. Right decisions come from here, your thinking center, not your head. This is the area where the soul makes peace just before returning home from its visit to earth. The center of all communication. The center of your being.

The visualization of yellow and this area, simultaneously, is beneficial in the digestive system and the releasing of body weight. Yellow's sister color, gold, is somewhat similar in one respect. A lemon-meringue yellow may represent illumination of the soul. Gold represents coming into the awareness of your spiritual power, in effect, the same meaning.

This area of the body has been referred to as the Lord God Of Your Being and where the soul dwells; although the seat of the soul being the center area of the brain, at the pineal body.

4th HEART CHAKRA, the color is green. The sound is FA in F; location, heart. "THE GLORY." This, our largest single energy center, is our center for healing and emits the color of growth, green. When fully operating, it promotes healing to the entire body. When open and balanced, it activates the immune and endocrine systems.

Meditation on this area releases one from self-hatred and the preprograms of unworthiness and helps to bring confidence and self-esteem. Meditating on and balancing this area may not help your spouse, parents, or children understand you, but is that your desire? I hope not. What a waste of what could be very productive meditation time. What happens here is the change of the only one you can change, YOU!

If you are still in that old-fashioned idea of getting others to understand you, it may be helpful if you rehearse this area of teaching with a friend. Meditating on this chakra will open your understanding towards others like you wouldn't believe. I speak from experience. You will soon find yourself allowing them what you previously would not allow. You know, things like freedom of speech, to be lively, lazy, personal opinions, choice of food, what "THEY" want to be when they "grow up," etc.

You release yourself of jealousy problems if you meditate on pink here to increase the love vibration while asking God to dip down His perfect love. I don't think you will overwork the guy. You may mentally spell out D-I-V-I-N-E L-O-V-E to yourself while focused here for even more of that kind of influence.

Imbedded in the central core of your heart, one sixteenth of an inch tall, is what has been titled, "The Three Fold Flame" or, your alter. Just by giving it thought makes it glow and expand. An affirmation for this is, "I open, balance, blaze, expand the three fold flame within my heart." This should be repeated no less than three times. Picture in your mind's eye, sitting on a throne in the center at the rear of your heart, making all your decisions from this area. You may get elaborate if you like. See yourself in a white silk robe with golden trim. Visualize yourself as a golden, glowing light within the robe.

5th THROAT CHAKRA. The color is blue. The sound is SO in G; location, thyroid area. "THE POWER." This is the area of your body of inner travel and meditation; to include dignity, pride, and dynamic action.

Meditate on this area as you visualize blue for enhancing the abilities of self expression, public speaking, communication, salesmanship, and negotiating skills with spouse. Go here to forgive self and others for ill-placed judgments. For heaven's sake (sake of the kingdom of God coming through your Christ consciousness), if you are harboring past resentments or revenges, STOP READING and go there now for a five-minute meditation. That kind of stuff can turn malignant.

By the way, if you don't immediately connect with any ill feelings toward others, consider the fact that in your subconscious mind, as we refer to it, which is the holding tank for most all of your conditions, it might be a condition or conditions that you are consciously unaware of. Then you dare say, "Yeah, but you don't know how badly that beastly jerk has done me wrong." Consider this, if God won't change the jerk, think you will? I refer to the only mind that you have any power on earth or heaven to change—YOURS.

If you happen to be in the mindset that the internal dispersing of hatred toward "the jerk" is gonna' change him or gratify you spiritually, I have important news for you. By harboring the attitude of hatred in the cellular structure of the human anatomy, you literally are decomposing and causing the destruction of cells of the body, as alcohol does to the cells of the brain. You therefore lose energy and gain age.

When others wrong you, welcome it, go within and ask, "What is this here to teach me?" Be brave as Daniel in the den of lions and be open as the flower that always welcomes that li'l guy with the stinger that brings her the source of procreation. Otherwise, you're gonna' develop a lethal case of *hardening of the attitudes*, and collapse your chance for super-consciousness.

What this oral reprimand has to do with your throat chakra is this: This is the area from which your power of meditation may manifest your heart's desires and from which you may consciously and endlessly view and travel through untold dimensions of universe. Been there, done that and let me say, "It's as different from watching THE BOX as hell is from heaven."

Tell-A-Vision, go inside and tell your own vision. The second coming is happening NOW. It is not something you will view on the TV. Be as the flower, open thyself to your high personal Self. Christ is not a last name to a man nor a certificate you hang on your wall to view. Christ is the God in you, in action, as soon as you set aside the ol' traditional ego.

6th BROW CHAKRA. The color is indigo. The sound is LA in A; location, at the brow of the forehead. Your spiritual power. This is the location of your pituitary gland, third eye. This eye! The light of the body is the eye. "If, therefore, thine eye be single, thy whole body shall be full of light."

This is how you can experience the Shekinah Glory. Meditation here activates the pituitary gland, which releases hormones/razon/ prana and/or what you may call monadic essence or Holy Spirit into the body.

Some characteristics here are beauty, friendliness, generosity, forgiveness, radiance, and happiness. Meditate here to release yourself from worry, anxiety, and fear-based emotional influences. This is your window into the most powerful nation on our planet, YOUR IMAGI-NATION.

7th CROWN CHAKRA. The color is white. The sound is TI

(pronounced tee) in B; location, top center of the head. "THE KING-DOM." Your personal connecting link with God. The color and chakra of divine truth and has been titled the sacred lotus blossom with one thousand petals, mostly white with hues of gold and lavender.

Meditations on this area begin instantly to raise your vibrational level from fear to love, bondage to freedom, illusion to truth. Relinquishes mental, emotional, and psychological negative conditions and brings self to a level of identity beyond physical limits at this energy vortex. Focusing your attention about an inch and a half above the top of the head, visualizing a pure white ray or shaft of light entering the top of the head as the sacred lotus blossom gently opens. Imagining the light penetrate and stimulate the pineal body in the center of the brain (what Webster refers to as the seat of the soul) will assist in the process of raising Kundalini to its full expression of life. Seek ye first this, "THE KINGDOM."

This area also enhances aspirations, inspiration, soul evolution, cosmic awareness and idealization.

May the Light be with you.

CHAPTER 14

Activating Your Auric Sight

Your ability to view auras is but one of your many God-given abilities. The reason most humans do not see auras is exactly the same reason most humans are far from wealthy. Guidance by exterior influence rather than interior influence; lack, want, limitation, manipulation, control, coercion, persuasion, ritual, tradition, stop, don't, can't, impossible, sit, stand, shut up, bug off, get lost, it's hard, it's difficult, this is good, this is bad, this is right, this is wrong, you're a bad li'l person, you're retarded, I can't make ends meet, that's evil.

Just as real as these words are to your eyes right now, they have preconditioned, unconditioned and/or conditioned your life or subconscious mind to the level of acceptance you had at the time they were administered to you, from now as you read this, to as far back as when you arrived from Mama.

That is just this one lifetime, and if you remain with the idea that God only gives you or allows you one trip—good for you! Look at the damage so far. It is okay with me if you stick with that extremely limited belief system because it may encourage you to get it right this trip. "It is appointed unto man to die but once," not live but once. There is a clue here, if you can hear me.

That is the outer ego, false self, that must die in order that you might break this continuous cycle of the wheel of birth and death in this physical state of limitations. Just because you believe not in multi-incarnations, doesn't make them go away. You can exist on the material planes and experience, through them, without being limited to them or imprisoned on them. If your mind is opened and your body relaxed, you will acquire profound truths from one end to the other of this material. Trust you. Your enlightenment is near.

Everyone and everything that has an atomic structure has an aura. The more dense the matter, such as rock or metal, etc., the less visible or detectable the aura. This is because the vibratory frequency is at a lesser cycle or lower rate. The higher the vibration, the more spiritual the color. From the low vibes of red to the high vibes of violet, gold and white, the highest frequency and the closest to pure, positive SOURCE ENERGY. The varied colors and size of the aura will distinguish personality, character, general thought patterns, health and well-being of the individual.

Scientists have researched and developed ways of capturing the aura on film and now even video. Reports of photographing the auric field extend back as far as 1890. Then in the 40's came the research and development of what is called Kirlian Photography by the soviet scientist husband and wife team, Semyon and Valentina Kirlian.

Science describes the process this way. The electric field causes the object being photographed to give off electrons. These are accelerated by the electric field and collide with molecules of air, causing the molecules to separate into positive oxygen, nitrogen ions, charged particles, and electrons. After a sufficient amount of positive ions have built up, the electrons and ions recombine, this recombination gives off emissions of ultraviolet light and that is how it shows up on a photograph—a bit technical, eh?

Because of this research, we are now able to diagnose disease and evaluate psychological states in color which, read with understanding of the meanings of color, shade, position, etc., can be very accurate. The larger, brighter, or more clear the aura, the healthier the body and mind of the eminator.

Now that you know how cameras pick up the auric field and that it is a "scientific fact" and they are real things, let's discover how to activate *your* auric vision. Activating your auric sight, lesson A, and the only lesson you may need in the matter if you apply the age-old ingredient that bars nearly everything when not applied.

This is not a course in development. It is a course in awakening, a reactivation of your mind. An activity that is fully alive and well just on the other side, higher side, of the part of the mind that is transporting the feedback to the brain so it may in turn assimilate, evaluate, analyze and conceptualize these words you are gazing upon now. Because of this process of potential consciousness, you are limited to what you perceive according to what you believe, "you will see it when you believe it."

Now here we are getting closer. Before going on, stop here, sit up straight, find yourself in comfort, take a deep, smooth breath in through the nose to the count of 5 or 6. As you let it out, count down from 8-7-6-5-4-3-2-1-zero. Now let your mind take you back to a very young age and a time when Mommy or Daddy were there to fulfill your every need, when you felt security (If that has never been true, imagine it so for a minute). "Only as a child shall you enter the gates of the higher dimensions." Now you can and will begin to see auras, with the application of the age-old ingredient, FAITH, and know the most powerful way to turn on to your auric sight.

Pause, be still, and now...

LOOK AT THEM!

Maybe not easy, but extreme simplicity. Get around others who either see auras, believe in them, or are at least very open to the fact that every "thing" is energy and glows; otherwise, cast not your potential pearls before swine (humans without a clue). When around those who are open of the mind, talk auras; feel theirs, touch theirs, sense it, smell it, play with it. Slap it around a little, guess their colors, have them guess yours. Bring the idea to life in your mind and your body will follow along because it believes everything you tell it.

Bring yourself into the moment—present time is the secret key to clairvoyance. Tell yourself I am right here, right now. Verbally give yourself permission to see auras, until you have gained 100% permission from within.

It may assist you to place your own personal movie screen about a foot in front of your forehead "The mind's eye" and allow yourself to see images or colors on it.

Get into your body. Exercise, deep breath for it, and for goodness sake put stuff that has life in it.

Give your body massages, hugs and make it feel wanted, appreciated, loved, and cared for. Your body is, in fact, your vehicle which you sense-perience life through.

Learn to validate your imagination. Imagination means seeing things in your mind's eye, which is a form of clairvoyance.

Seeing your aura is informative and life-affirming. It can change your whole perception on what is truly meaningful in life, and can open a window on your relationships with others.

One short simple exercise is to have a victim, I mean a friend, standing 10–15 feet away from you and two feet in front of a light-colored wall. Have them use their mind actively reciting the alphabet backwards or counting in threes or the like. The idea is to provoke thought.

Focus on the wall behind them, not on them. It's kinda' like diverging the sight as you would in the magic eye illusions books or pictures. Viewing just beside their neck, but focused on the wall.

Happy aura sightings to ya'!

CHAPTER 15

A Shade Between

Between black and white or between the colors of the rainbow, red and blue, there is a shade that often includes a dab of pink, but is the more basic color of magenta. I feel this shade deserves a bit of recognition because it frequently glows from the human, more often from the top right side of the head, as far down the body as the right hip or lower, depending on how much of the energies it represents are being sent out. The particular attributes of this pink-magenta shade are of the nature of affection, passion, emotional turn-on, and/or sensual stimuli.

One day I was positioned way in 'da back of a popular metaphysical bookstore in Springfield, Missouri. As I looked up to see what rang the front door entry chimes, I noticed there to be, walking my way just bigger than Dallas, a cowboy. By now I'm figuring it's just something in my karma. I mean Indians sure, but cowboys in a metaphysical bookstore? Then seeing his li'l lady with him, I just figured he's keeping an eye on her so's a crystal ball or witch's spell didn't fall on her.

Well, foiled again in my judgment. This guy was not only hip on the spiritual side of life, but knew a bit about the human aura as well; not to mention he was leading her.

They walked right up to me and my camera and he said, "Howdy, I'd like to get a picture of my 'filly' and I separately; then one of us together."

This being about the third time I'd been out with the aura camera, I was sure glad this guy knew what I was doing. After I completed their individual shots, I had them both sit together on the photo chair.

Only one chair can be used in this type of photography so she took his lap. I was trying to decide the next step of how to prepare them for the picture. As with one person, I will normally direct a short meditation, like hypnotic suggestions, for relaxing the client in order to see their most natural colors, aura, or mind set.

I certainly didn't contemplate long, as the cowboy raised his hand facing the camera saying, "Wait before you shoot. We would like to prepare for this shot."

As they began to embrace, ever so gently; it led to a bit more aggressive involvement, then progressively evolved to a most passionate entanglement, to a downright "R" rated display of sensual correspondence. I mean, people were linin' up admiring the show sayin' things like, "We'll be next!"

I peeled off the back of the first picture I took, which was hers. She had an abnormal amount of pink on her right side. This side representing the sending out of energies. I looked over to him and said, "I think she likes me… pause… and it's possible she even likes you a little bit too" as we all got a laugh out of my ever-so-brilliant sense of humor.

As I opened his photo, we viewed a most amazing phenomena. He had as large an amount of pink as she did, but on his left side; indicating the recipient of such energies, which is affection. Now mind ya' here, this couple, at this point of having each of their photos taken, were not yet into the let's say, "emotional turn-on mode." I looked at him and said, "Someone here is really liken' you a lot. I know I like you, but I didn't think that much, so it's possible, as I glanced toward his beautiful wife, that someone else here likes you too!"

Of course, we all got another laugh from that one.

I looked at them and said, "Ya' know, I'm getting the sensation of a close connection here. Never have I seen this much pink around a married couple before."

Normally the younger couples I meet are not only un-affectionate towards each other, but more often, by far, I see a muddy blackish red or greenish yellow or brown around 'em; indicating, to say the least, a definite lack in negotiating skills or a case of the who's-gonna'-be-the-most-right-tonight blues. It was quite obvious to the trained eye that this couple was a "get along" kinda' team.

I truly enjoyed meeting them and hope they get a copy of this book. I didn't get their names.

I suppose you're wondering about that third together shot? Well, as I opened the third photo of them posing together—real together—we once again viewed an amazing phenomena. The pink over either side of them had moved together and intensified in size and changed to a beautiful shade of pink mixed with magenta; which I will now, for future reference, title "pinkgenta."

After explaining the colors to them, and the special closeness these colors represent, she pulled me to the aisle, away from the crowd, and said, "You know you are so right about us. There is something special about our relationship, I mean really special. I truly believe we are soul mates, you know."

I looked at her and said, "I don't think so," as "he" stepped over to us. "I've studied the nature of the spirit, soul, body and mind of mankind for many years and come across much on the subjects of the soul of the mineral, vegetable, and animal kingdoms. They are all inner-related to each other by way of a group soul, where the human has obtained to the level of an individualized soul or one of free will, God over his/her own life."

Now at this point it is of tremendous importance for the reader to understand that "individualized" and "separated" mean NOT the same thing. There is only one true separation from anything and that is the imagination of separateness in consciousness. One can imagine their way to separation—as lethal as death to the embodiment—or imagine oneness to such a degree as to send the idea of separateness back to the nothingness from whence it came. More on this later. For now, I didn't leave the couple hangin' for long after saying I did not think that they were soul mates.

I looked at him and said, "You two have an unusually rare bond for eartheans." As I shifted my eyes to hers, I asked, "Have you ever heard the term "twin flames?"

You woulda' had to been there, viewing the countenance upon their faces, as their jaws went down and eyebrows reached for the sky, to see what seemed as a profound memory of a past life simultaneously experienced. I do believe a memory bell did sound in their minds at the mention of the term twin flames.

I went on to explain that we have many soul mates on earth, some more in tune with others; parents, children, friends and/or lovers may be your soul mates, but twin flames—you have but one. It is rare indeed that you would both incarnate on earth at the same frame of time. I said, "If you are, as it seems, twin flames, since you have met, being separated again would not become a negotiation. Divorce shall never enter your minds for any reason." They affirmed this to be true.

Rent the movie "Somewhere in Time," with Christopher Reeves for a profound reference on close souls or see "Titanic."

If you are this couple I speak of, please send me a copy of your photos for a later book and if you like, your names as well.

For more information on twin flames, read *2150 AD.* by Thea Alexandra. In her novel, she explains the reality quite well. I believe her novel ideas are to become a most likely experience of our future, and hopefully, her book a made into a movie.

I have deliberately turned ladies on, with their permission, by whispering in their ear with my impression of Elvis, as an experiment, just before taking their picture. In many of these cases, if the effect is received properly, their photo comes out a bright magenta or pinkgenta on the right side. Showing this color represents emotional turn-on.

Now I would like to share a more hit-home kinda' story of an esoteric nature for planetary educational purposes regarding a shade between red and white.

There is a major shortage of pink on this planet and it seems to be on a rapid decline. What can be done about it? You can start by trusting yourself and others instead of fighting and resisting what they do. If you're gonna' fly banners, do it on behalf of love, not against evil. As you resist evil, you submit to fear of it. You say to it, "Yes Evil, you have power over me, so if we get rid of you, I can get my power back."

Let me ask you, if you never leave home, how can you experience being in other places/happenings? Experience is only a vacation away from home. It cannot harm the real you in any way. I said, "REAL YOU." Isn't it wonderful to return home after a trip away? EVIL is merely the opposite magnetic energy of polarity that allows spirit to LIVE away from its true nature, identity, or home. Why give your power away to something created so you may have an experience away from home? Instead of a banner for evil, be one for love— which is the higher choice!

You can also be of tremendous assistance, in more pink, by "letting" people on the road rather than flipping people off. If we don't start turning our planet pink, it will be done for us.

There was once a group of several brave souls who incarnated on this planet not long ago. The reason they came may become obvious to you if you listen to that small inner voice deep within your heart. Go ahead, 60 seconds of your precious 24-hour day, this will strongly enhance the comprehension of the message herein.

Now take a deep, smooth breath. As you release, verbally or mentally, ask the universe to bring you understanding. Now breathe in understanding as you focus your attention well within the center of your heart.

Back to the story. As the brave souls sat in council with their overlords, they responded to the proposed mission, "Yes, we see if we do this, at this time, on our own planet, how it will help accelerate compassion and stimulate the feeling of the need for change with our earth brothers and sisters."

Then the overlord spoke, "Do you see how this will bring the free country back towards their original purpose as caretakers of the beloved Goddess Mother Earth?"

"Yes we do, and we will be with those members of our soul family for that moment in time. Yes, Father (Source), these roles we play will turn a great number of hearts pink. When can we go?"

The angels began to sing and the guides prepared to descend with the selected souls. The heavens opened for delivery as the volunteers began to incarnate into their mortal vehicles for their mission. One by one, month by month, year by year, they descended to assume their individual roles.

The inner purpose was all but erased from memory as the normal process of earth life has it. Some grew to maturity, others just arrived. God's perfect plan was in order for all the world to see.

Finally that glorious day of a great awakening, the day that most of the souls return home to Source, except the ones who loaded and parked the truck. They would remain to experience the judgment they had previously placed on others.

April 19, 1995, Oklahoma City, Oklahoma. After the bombing turned the Federal building red, the media sent out the message that turned the hearts of the planetary inhabitants pink. Mission accomplished. Thank you "up there" volunteers, we'll see you soon.

We do, in fact, have a shortage of pink on this gorgeous planet. Just because we are not using it, doesn't mean it isn't there to be used. There is not, was not, and never will there be a shortage of divine love. But if you don't use it, how can you have it?

The cosmic clock is bringing us to a new age of enlightenment; one that you may join if your vibration is compatible with the higher vibrations of love. It is your choice brother/sister. This kind of information, out to all now, is the wake-up call for atonement (at-one-ment).

God's law allows everything; man's law seeks to control everything. God's law protects; man's law kills. God's law is perfect; man's law... O.J. trial!????? I judge not a man, everyone has their roles to play out and some are more eye-opening and are brought for every eye to see. Man's law can be purchased to fulfill a desire, want, or need. God's law fulfills all needs and is available only through vibrational harmony with it.

There is another "shade between" that I would like to share. This one between black and white, closest to yellow, the color of communication. I was in Sedona photographing people's auras. As I was explaining the gold around a client, a young lady, a nurse, stepped forward with a comment. "That's the color I see when you make peace."

We both looked her way as I said, "Excuse me, what do you mean?"

She explained, saying, "One day, I was with a lady patient who was due for surgery. Her vital signs were all good enough for it. As I was examining her, all of a sudden, out from her midsection; solar plexus, came a beautiful gold, rising up like a child playing ghost under a sheet. The most pure, bright, golden color I have ever witnessed raised up and surrounded her whole body, then like a vacuum pulling from the solar plexus, withdrew back into her. There was no question for me as to the meaning of this."

As the doctor entered, ordering the patient to be taken for surgery, I exclaimed, "She won't be joining us for surgery, doctor! "

As he checked her blood pressure and noted the good heartbeat pattern, he asked, "What are you talking about? This patient is fine for surgery."

I retorted, "She's already made peace."

As the doctor rudely ordered her to be brought to the surgery room, the patient expired before reaching the door of the room she was in.

A note to the medical institutions of our planet. Know this administrators, doctors, and all who care, to include the drug companies; if you are in it for the human, my admiration goes out to you. May you live in the countenance of next step rather than next stress. I understand that you cannot be absolute about every surgery or prescription that you administer, those are not the ones I speak of.

From here, you being the ten-year students, intellectually adept, you may fill in the "what I'm indicating," blanks yourself as you so cleverly read between the lines. This planet and all the humans upon her who adapt to the vibration of love are graduating to something much higher than what you can acquire in the academic structures developed by man, with or without you. In the higher vibrations, selfish ends will not exist, so if that's your intent, you cannot exist there either.

A brief message to the doctor who has been referred to as the one who goes around "acting like God." What those who use this metaphor to express your character more specifically mean, in a more accurate description, is that you are going around acting like a "control freak."

Let me ask you, have you looked up the word "doctor" in your Webster? I mean, you do go by the "book" do you not? You should find it twice; in part, the first meaning says; to teach; under the second meaning; 1B, to restore to good conditions; and 2B, to alter deceptively. Which of the B categories do you FALL under, huh Doc,? Is it 2B or not 2B?

Soon we will be viewing the colors around each other and that's why this book is in your hands. You shall be known by the colors you emit. What colors do you resonate to? Love is in many colors, but the shades are pure.

May pink—a shade between—befall the world. Affection.

CHAPTER 16

Touched by An Angel

"Happiness is a perfume you cannot pour on others
without getting a few drops on yourself."

–Ralph Waldo Emerson

ack in the early 90's, I established an office supply company in Nixa, Missouri. "The classiest, most plush of them all," claimed Steve K., the National Sales Rep for United Stationers, one of the largest office stationery supply companies in the world.

The credit for the design, esthetics, and formatting of the company goes to the president of the corporation, my former wife, who spent many long days and nights setting up the files, shelves, office, work areas, counters, computers, vendors, employing help, purchasing products, and establishing services that the company would provide; not to mention the long list of all the things she did that I haven't mentioned.

Up to this point, I had established 12 businesses. The last six of which began to show a profit in three months time. We successfully sold these businesses within 11 months of opening them. I say we, my brother, John, and I were business partners for a number of years. The intent behind the establishing and selling of these businesses (auto repair shops) was to eventually become franchisors of business. However, I found myself attempting to live someone else's dream.

I was a very good salesman for the companies, the best, but a prudent businessman NOT! It was my brave brother, John, who possessed the "make it happen" attitude. I suppose this is due to the Aries in him. He knew when to buy and sell and get in and out. We finally parted ways. I think he knew his goals of life. I did not know mine.

My life was not what I wanted it to be. Over the six or seven years I spent working with brother John, I was fairly oblivious to a quality of consciousness that I did not possess, but was quite aware of the fact that John had it deeply imbedded within himself. COMPASSION—something I didn't express often to the humans who came to our shops with blown engines or transmissions.

John expressed a true empathy toward these situations. I expressed more along the lines of how much it's gonna' set you back to repair that auto you've been abusing. It took more than all the small claims cases I went through to get it through to me that I lacked compassion.

One day, as I was altercating with my wife at the office supply store in the latter part of our daily disagreement, she loudly and firmly, as she reorganized her desk with one single swoop, stated, "YOU HAVE NO COMPASSION!"

I kinda' shut up, thinking, gee I never quite heard it put that way before. Was John my example, angel of compassion? Was my wife my teaching angel of compassion? I had no rebut to my wife's statement. I just contemplated on it for hours.

Then the days passed, I still had this thought, "I lack compassion for humans," therefore, I lack in a major Godly quality. As the weeks passed, I continued to cogitate this all-powerful statement made with the emotion (energy in motion) of "anger," but the utmost sincerity. I knew she was serious because of the way she performed that spring cleaning thing with her desk and it wasn't even spring time.

My life was a disaster, everything about it. You know how it feels when you are baking a cake, fixing a meal, repairing an auto, and you are missing an important ingredient, tool, part, or some one thing needed to complete your project? Sure you do! Well, my life felt as if I had one empty bowl—no ingredients to bake anything with. I needed to turn to something for help and religion was not my number one choice since I had enough of that crammed down my throat as a child, which certainly didn't bring me to any abundant ways of experiencing my visit to our lovely planet.

When I was about 14, I got so upset with my idea of some big bad dude on a throne wearing a huge golden crown with lots of stars, I actually challenged him to come on down and duke it out.

I was working on a go-cart I bought for five dollars. My mechanical dexterity skills were not doing so well. I told that guy in the sky it was His fault—He put me here in the first place. All I ever heard in church was, He's gonna send me to hell if I don't get right with Him here.

At that moment I knew there wasn't anything going right anyway, so if He was going to do that later, then it was time now to do something about it. I said, after calling Him a few choice names,

"You come on out from behind those clouds, quit hiding behind your throne and let's have it out right here and now!"

I was definitely not in a good mood. I was ready to float like a butterfly and sting like a bee. I just figured He knew it because He, as usual, was a no-show.

Well, later I cooled down and felt all that shame, guilt, and fear stuff so I apologized to God and told His son that I didn't mean any of that stuff I said about His pop.

Long about the age of twenty, an acquaintance gave me a book title, *ESP*, by Harold Sherman. It got me started on a path of understanding about this "God thing." This book was easy for me to grasp its simplistic terms. By the way, besides *Black Beauty*, back in school, it was the first book I ever read cover-to-cover. It was so logical, it created in me a profound interest. Over the next few years, I acquired my own li'l library of metaphysical books.

Word gets around, especially within family; it got around to mine. Some were okay with my interest, others had their opinions and no less than one family member had big-time judgment about my "other than standard, orthodox fundamental belief system."

Some of my family have been praying for my salvation. They seem pretty sure that because I do not go to church, I will burn. At this point I would like to thank them for their prayers and, in their way, love towards me. Thank you Father and thank you li'l sis. Now back to opinions. I have one of my own—here's mine.

I think some people believe themselves to be good Christians for various reasons, many different reasons. Here's one: I heard many people referred to as good Christians by the "PR" people, pastors and administrators of the organized religious structures. That's good PR work and/or salesmanship on their part. It helps to keep the foundation together and is an excellent reinforcement of job security for the administrators.

What used to puzzle me though was when they would tell their members that the Lord appreciates their financial support and without it, His house, churches, could not exist. The donators would be rewarded accordingly in heaven, not now, always LATER.

Now help me out here on this part. When Sunday came, the PR guy would get up and preach that money and getting into those pearly gates of heaven are not compatible in the least; then pass the plate, "Get rid of that evil stuff." I certainly understand the motive with this, up to here, but this is where I get confused. They would receive this evil stuff that keeps you out of heaven, and even beg for more of it by telling stories of poor li'l ol' ladies who gave all their money and the baseball players who gave 90% of theirs.

If you don't take money to heaven when you go because they don't use it there, then what in heaven's name does financially supporting earthly institutions have to do with going to, or in the more accurate sense, arriving into the state of heaven?

One of the most excellent examples of the religious public relations officer's (pastor's) manipulations with either BS or ignorance on their part is this. They read it right from the book of course, and Matthew, Mark, and Luke did jot it down but it's now at least one word off. "It is easier for a camel to go through 'the eye of a needle,' than for a rich man to enter into the kingdom of God." After reciting this to their flock they would then urge you with a li'l guilt and shame about that evil stuff and before you know it, here comes the deacons with the plate.

However, the truth of this is that when Jesus was giving an example of our attachment to material things to his disciples as written in Matthew, He used "The eye of <u>the</u> needle" as a metaphor. NOTE: The key word here is attachment, not material. "They" (translators) changed "the" to "a." If you desire proof of this, the gate of the wall that surrounds Jerusalem still exists and the name of this gate is "The Eye of The Needle." Here's the reason it acquired such a name: Back then, if you were well-off and moving to Jerusalem with a caravan of camels loaded with all your stuff, the camels had to be unloaded to pass under the gate because there is a top over it. You can see the difficulty here. It was not easy for the camels to pass through. Just as your attachment to the material makes it difficult to seek God or the process of ascension.

ATTENTION ALL EARTHEANS! This is a special report to help you remember who you really are. Money doesn't bring you to, or keep your from, heavenly awareness. Institutions don't get you there; even God Himself, or His son, don't bring you there.

The choice to get there is made by the one and only who chose to come here; unless you wanna blame God for your being here. Free will zone means it is only by your choice that the veil be lifted. You are the only one who can make this selection.

You say, how? That is what this book, and so many like it, are here for, but you must accept for self. Just as a radio receives from many broadcasting stations, you still must select the station you wish to be in harmony with. The Kingdom of God is of a high vibration, "the highest." The vibration is love, opposite of fear. You must intentionally tune your body and mind to the channel to which you wish to resonate. You must tune your heart and mind to the most powerful of all vibrations—the vibration of unconditional or divine love.

There are many scriptures of old that were written so the writer wouldn't get stoned; therefore, difficult to decipher. Regardless, much of it is simply put across to us the way "THEY" want us to see it. Many books on the subject of reincarnation were stricken, primarily for THEIR selfish reasons.

I often get the distinct feeling as I discuss the subject with nonbelievers, that they do not believe in reincarnation simply because they are afraid the next time around would likely be the same as the one they are now experiencing. Why they think that hell is down there when they are living it here is beyond me; but with these attitudes of fear and resistance, you can be relatively sure that the next life will include, but not be limited to, very similar experiences.

Do you truly believe that a being, capable of creating six billion souls (our population now), is also capable of creating one hundred billion, maybe one hundred trillion souls, but not capable of giving an individual soul more than one visit to this beautiful planet? What about the infant who lives but a year or two? That's it? Last chance? Final incarnation? Where do all the souls come from? Why do they get but one chance to get it right, be saved, or burn in hell forever? Why a new soul for each and every body? Think you have experienced God's whole intended process in but one single visit? Religious or metaphysical, you sure want to believe this be your final earth trip, huh? I mean, we have eternity, but no chance of RE-incarnation, no-o-o-o, just once, right? Give me a break! If you don't believe it, it doesn't exist, right? But if that is true, the same is true about what you do believe does exist and you have made it quite clear to me that you do believe in HELL and its leader, "THE DEVIL."

I challenge you to see what is backwards in anyone's belief system who believes in THE DEVIL and that is what they did backwards. Now spell that speck of no-thing-ness backwards, "LIVED." When you reverse this word, you have two Gods. You tell me you believe in only one. Excuse me folks, I had to bitch-out my li'l sis for lettin' those organizations lead her into those awful illusions of fear.

Every so often, I will return to the story at hand. If there is anything I can say along the way to assist you in remembering who you are, you can bet I will. And by the way, I do not let my subject interfere with what I have to say.

Back to that office supply company. It was just one of the areas of my life that wasn't going according to plan. We had already owned it for nearly two years and tried to convey it, since it's conception, with no luck. I applied all the methods that sold our houses and businesses prior, but none worked. I hired brokers and ran ads in different publications month after month. Finally I got out of the papers. The contracts with all brokers had expired. I decided no one else is gonna change my life, so I better do it myself. But how?

I had been doing positive affirmations for months, till my face turned blue. I had been doing mantras. I had been praying and working hard, very hard, and just barely paying the bills. One day, after one of those major heated, conditional negotiations with my partner that never go well, I decided I would dedicate myself to a minimum of one hour of meditation every morning and just do it until change happened or until I discovered it just didn't work.

I recalled some very impressive upliftments and improvements that mediating brought me in years past. That was ten years ago and I had been busy working for money, no time for serious meditations.

I followed through. I would open the store each morning at 8:00 AM, but I would get there between 6:00-7:00 AM and begin my morning meditation. Three weeks passed and a phenomenon happened. Now mind you here, the business had not been listed for months. I was waiting on a lady at the counter and we got to talking and she mentioned that she and her husband were from Colorado and they were headed to Missouri.

"How's business down here in Nixa?" she asked.

I replied, "growing," which was obvious, Nixa was one of the fastest growing towns in Missouri at the time.

Through the conversation, she learned that we were offering our business for sale. The next morning, I stopped by my favorite li'l farm boy restaurant to have some vittels on my way to town for supplies and guess who was sitting there having breakfast? The lady from Colorado and her husband. We talked for a while and then I had to go. I knew one part of Missouri they would like was that li'l down-home cookin', inexpensive restaurant, The Sale Barn. The food was good—the best.

To brief this part of the story, the lady called my wife that afternoon to ask her if our store was for sale. She was soon to be a qualified CPA and her husband was a printer. They were a perfect match for our business. This was the first business I had ever sold where the buyer's offer was the same as my initial asking price.

I began to become just a little more conscious of life as it happened around me while I continued to force myself to mediate daily, every morning and most nights. I never missed morning meditations. This continued for five months. No longer was it force.

As a matter of fact, as I began to travel with my new career, I would go to Sedona. I had the opportunity to stay for two months during one period and go into the mountains between work hours. I found myself meditating up to eight hours a day on occasion and never less than three. So far the most important thing I have learned about meditating is to do it! At least 20 minutes a day. I do not recommend eight hours. I am an experimental kinda guy. The most proper style, way, or method does not have as much bearing as to just do it! Because when you sit and still your body you will be guided on how, when, where, etc.

Before training was over for the new owners of what used to be Porter Office Supply, now B.O.S.S. Office Supply in Nixa, Missouri, I began to view life just a little differently. One day it dawned on me that I was viewing life from a different plateau. I began to notice things in a different light.

I used to think the people around Springfield, Missouri were mean and mad because someone had stolen those three missing girls. I would go to the major office supply stores for the products we didn't buy from other distributors or factories. I had made friends with several of the employees. I noticed on my several hundred trips up to

Springfield that the general population was not outwardly expressing anything similar to happiness. Well, it finally came to my awareness what could have been causing all these humans to be in the mindset of living hell.

When we first moved, with our li'l farts, to Nixa, Missouri, my wife got a bug up her gluteus maximus and decided that we, having young children, should take them to a house of organized religion. But when that guy in the suit got behind the pulpit and started yelling at all of us; calling us sinners and unworthy, that we should feel guilt and shame, my wife had a quick change of mind, grabbed the kids and said aloud, "I am not going to let that man call my children names," as she took their hands and we walked out.

We discovered that the activity in that particular building was what could be summed up as the local organized teachings for various states of self-denial or seminars and workshops of the true hellfire and brimstone. Their motto or mission statement, "If we're going down, let's take you too!" or "Hell is only a thought away." Could I do wonders for their Sunday bulletin or what?

Well, I came to the understanding of why all those folks I would see shopping at the store, were walking around looking like they had been visiting Lucifer's crash pad. They had been getting it dumped on 'em in the name of the Lord on a weekly or biweekly basis and had to pay for it to boot. Imagine how profoundly ridiculous this sounds.

You go to an organization that is supposed to lift you or assist in such and teach you things like walking on water. That's what His boy said, right? "Even greater things you shall do," but instead of teaching you your equality with the master and oneness with His universe, no-o-o-o, they treat you like a garbage can with a hairy lid. When they get done dumping their garbage on you, instead of paying the normal hauling away fees, they tell you that you gotta give 10% of your earnings or you risk the long-term burn! Hasn't this kind of abuse to our earth family members gone just about far enough?

I was shopping at one of my favorite office supply companies where the employees excelled in good ol' fashioned friendly, down home kinda' service. One afternoon, I noticed the normal amount of smiles on the customer's faces, NONE! This store's personnel had always performed a most efficient job of providing me with special orders and having, in most cases, the stock of my needs and excellent personnel service. They just liked me better than the other customers, right? I think not. I observed the way in which they treated their customers; kind and courteous. It was incredulous how so many faces gave impressions like, "prices too high," "service too low," "they're just out to get me and make me buy their stuff," "it's cheaper at that other store, but they are always out of what I want," and "I always have to stand in line here, why can't they get some more help around here?"

It seemed obvious that these humans were going biweekly to one of those good ol' organizations where one a' them *loud speakers* gets up in front and starts yellin' and callin' 'em names like; "you unworthy sinners." Maybe these customers were just expressing, through their countenance, the previously imposed round of guilt, shame, and need to repent their evil ways from last Sunday's service. Whatever you call it, when li'l hypnotized sheep are subjected to an onslaught of more hypnotic suggestions of self-denial, rather than self worth.

The problem with some of these methods of sharing the "word " is the way in which that "inspired word" becomes twisted toward the intent of the sharer of the message, you know the guy, 99% of the time GUY. The one up there thumping the book, yelling, "It's all in the book" and then it's like he read the book and claims to understand it.

Well, I have read the Bible and it's too bad the Englishmen, "control freaks," did in fact, get hold of it. Fortunately there remains some truth in it but even that has been diluted. You need not read between the lines; however, to see the many references the Bible makes to the fact that "IT IS ALL IN YOU" ! ! It's not the book or the planet that goes on forever, but the vibration of thought of source. "MY WORD REMAINETH." "BY MY WORD THIS ALL EXISTS" and by your words, your life is what it is today.

The book, as Jesus was pointing out to the local rock throwing group, His followers, "Jesus answered them, Is it not written in your law, I said, Ye are all Gods," (John 10:34) but no-o-o-o, they later got that big G outta' there and gave it a little g. Then they took the greatest master ever sent to enlighten them from their pithy ignorance up the hill and murdered Him.

Some say that if Jesus had not been murdered, we could never be saved. I sincerely claim that had we not murdered Him, most of us would be walking on water by now. He was teaching us that we are all Gods, right? If you wish to white out this big G and insert a small g, do it in your own book. I will stay with the big one until I arrive at that awareness, thank you!

Do you know the difference between a big shot and a little shot? A big shot is a little shot that just kept on shootin'.

How could you ever expect to smell roses if you continue to return to someone who uses you for a garbage can with a hairy lid? Until you remove yourself from this negative vibrational frequency, you will not be capable of getting the message that GOD, CHRIST, HOLY SPIRIT, and HEAVEN are not a person, place or thing you may earn now for later, if you pass the pre-qualifications.

Oh eartheans, the wake-up call is here and now! If you cannot hear it with the ear, can you feel it deep inside your midsection or possibly in the depth of your heart? The "I AM," the great "I AM Presence" or WHO YOU BE is pressing out to know, to become, to be you.

God's original plan for the garden of Eden, the entire earth, may come into expression and return to its pristine beauty, only through the atonement (at-one-ment) with Him, by becoming. Yes, we have free will and most continue "not to be." We are all the fragmented souls of but one body. Jesus was not the only one to be Christ. He was our way-shower. Have you any idea how many times He recited the affirmations that brought Him to His level of illumination?

I found myself asking more questions about the mental and emotional condition of the customers at those big chain stores. On one visit, I was walking towards the counter for checkout and noticed a customer "coming down on" one of my favorite clerks, Linda. She handed him some papers to fill out and sign as she apologized on behalf of the store for his life becoming such a disaster from the products he purchased. I came in during the middle of this, but was paying close attention to the remainder of the role being played as I walked up to the counter with my cart.

Linda turned to serve the next customer, me, while the other customer was filling out his paperwork. She began to ring up my stuff as I loudly asked her one of my most common questions when I see her, and I must say the timing was perfect. As I shook her hand saying, "Good-day Linda. How are you treating earth life today?"

She said, "I'm doing the best I can. "

I asked, "Any customers smile upon you today?"

She said, "NO! "

I said, "So, could I assume that none of them have hugged you today?"

She said, "Good assumption."

I said, "Could I be safe in betting money that no one has kissed you today?"

As she went into store-wide noticeable laughter, she replied, "NO, NOT YET!"

Linda noticed the customer had completed the forms so she turned to his side of the counter to receive them and finalize the transaction. As the customer looked up at her, he said, "I overheard what was being said," as he glanced my direction and looked back to her, "and I feel bad about the way I treated you. I want to apologize for it."

Linda gave him a warm "thank you" as he rushed on out of the store. As Linda turned back to serve me, I looked at her and asked, "Linda, let me ask you why is it that, in spite of the non-smiling clientele here, every time I see you and Tamera, Dianna and Johnny, your faces are always smiling?"

She said, "That's because when you come in, you always say something to make us smile."

I replied, "So that's what does it, huh?"

Then with her eyes penetrating into mine, she paused, her visage, became sincere and poised as she calmly, with the most warm and gentle voice, said, "Yes, that and because you have been touched by an angel."

Dear reader, let me be as clear as I can be on the message herein.

Linda's statement not only made my day, week and month, but impacted my life with such a divine sensation of love that the influence of that short sentence continues to ring in my consciousness today and will continue to influence my life forevermore. There is the power of love within the contents of the sincere compliment. Do you ever know which one you give will be life-transforming unto the recipient?

Before I moved from Missouri, I made a special trip to that store where Linda, Tamera, Johnny, David, Jack, Rick, and Diana worked. I caught half of 'em there and said my good-byes. I noticed Linda's register without customers, I walked up, held my hand out to shake hers, I looked at her sincerely, as I held her hand softly, and told her I was moving away.

I then said Linda, "Do you recall the time you said I had been touched by an angel? Well, I was in fact touched by a real live angel."

She said, "You were, really?"

I replied, "Yes, I was indeed and that is why I came by so I could personally thank the angel who touched me."

Thank you Linda for allowing God's divine love to resonate through you. I will do what I can to find you so I can send you a copy of my book.

Remember Who You Are

CHAPTER 17

Unconditional Awareness

*He who knows others is clever;
he who know himself is enlightened.*

Lao-tse

n-conditionalization is ever present to behold; however, you may not receive what you do not give.

Your level of awareness is governed by your level of acceptance and allowance. To allow is to be like God, to accept is a preference. Allow everybody everything just as does God. Accept only what you prefer just as does Buddha. Now that you know the difference in allowance and acceptance, we can continue.

You cannot un-conditionalize another, but you can recondition your condition. When you first meet someone do you say, "Hello, I'm so-and-so, glad to change you." Of course not, but it is your intention, even if it is subconscious, in more cases than not. When you meet you may say, "Hello, I'm glad to meet you but I'm into unconditional relationships. I'll befriend you if we can have one of those." However, did you not just start this relationship out with your first condition?

There is but one way in which to un-conditionalize your relationships. You must become an unconditional individual. It may be true that your loving parents taught you love is conditional and it continues to be handed down from one generation to the next, until an individual decides not to be in acceptance of others' conditioning upon him. When love is allotted for trade, its nature of divinity is extracted, therefore it becomes a loveless trade.

Selfishness is an attitude that desires placement of conditions on others. You may easily realize that the most selfish of people place the most conditions on others. By conditionalizing others, you are animating the energies that you desire to live in within your world. If you dispute this, consider the meaning of the word "desire"—*give birth to*.

You choose daily the games of life you play and how you wish to play them. If on your playground of life all around you are family and friends under the influence of your attempt to control and condition them, consider this. You do have the freewill right to play the role of controller and conditioner. But as sure as the sun rises daily; whether or not in your view, the roles you create become the experience you will find yourself in, to the degree imposed by you. You have bound yourself to live under controlled, conditioned, condemnation by your own actions. The universal law of balanced proportion is that you must experience what you set in motion in its exact, full expression.

Let me break this down in simpler terms. The way in which you trick or treat others is the exact degree of your initiated intent of how you will be tricked or treated. Not just sorta, kinda, almost the same, but precisely, exactly—to the perfect measure, balance and polarity of how you think, speak and act toward other people, places, things; yes, inanimate objects, animals, plants, mother earth, food and the chair you sit in. You design your future in your present, you always have and you always will because you are a powerful creator.

So let me ask you, when is a good time to begin to pre-cast the kinda life that you prefer to live in? Know that even when your life is turned toward love, you will still meet up with all the energies you have set in motion. This may have become a very large snowball of negativities or evils. I know mine was, but I have a different snowball gradually growing and picking up speed along with its momentum and I'm not speaking figuratively when I say speed. Pouring out thanksgiving and divine or unconditional love, and a lot of "bless you's" is melting my 40-year-old snowball into the nothingness it was before I created it. Thank God it works! And honey, if it works for this guy, it will for anyone because you name it, "I've been there and done that" and I am not a quick learner so I've repeated the process many times.

Just attempt to give all your love away for one of your earth days, make no exceptions or conditions on who gets it. This part is of extreme importance. Do not analyze the would-be recipients, just aim and pour. I double dog dare ya'! If you do this, you have just claimed your inheritance of God for a day. If this doesn't quite fit some limited, conventional, orthodox, traditional, fundamental, establishmentarian, conformist belief system—well look it up—it's in the book, "GOD IS LOVE." One becomes that which one dispenses.

You don't correct relationships in the counselor's office and you don't make the corrections in others. Thank God for this realization! I've tried that, been there, it doesn't work. You must become, in yourself, the correction. If the shrinks of the world could actually cure you in your relationships, they would experience a major lack in job security. I've met with many professionals in the psychological field of counseling. Some speak from their hearts and some, in this academically structured society, certainly aced their "BS" degree. They could easily convert to a liar, I mean lawyer.

If we all went within to our hearts and the feelings that the almighty "I AM " presence continues to out-press upon us, we would shift the world's careers to some very wonderful and new experiences in the job market.

This chapter, by the way, is devoted to relationships and yet has not to do with any other but you. Of course, without the other, you have nothing to relate with or to. This was exemplified with profound simplicity when Ralph Cramden said to his wife Alice, "Alice, I'm the boss and you're nothing."

Alice replied, "Well Ralph, I guess that makes you the boss of nothing."

It is not the other we are assisting to change. If you've ever tried that, you already know it doesn't work. We are here to assist in the only one you can possibly make any changes in, YOU.

WHO YOU ARE NOT

Let me ask you something. If you drove through a red light, whether you meant to do it or not, then got pulled over and ticketed by a cop, would you blame it on God because He created you? I mean, He is your creator, right? None of this would have happened had He not created you, right?

Did you know that there are fathers and mothers on this planet who feel deeply responsible for the output of their offspring? Are you one?

I know one who actually believes in his conscience, that if his children don't make it to heaven, he is to blame and it will be his fault. This same man took it very personally when his li'l children would come home with low grades from school, act up in church, or cause trouble in the neighborhood, as if he did it himself. With one exception there was someone to correct for it. Correction stands out in the minds of some of this man's children far more real than his love or understanding ever did.

You may think here, "Well now David, it sounds like you haven't forgiven your father or you wouldn't be writing this memory of him." Well, I hope to heaven my heart is clear of my resentment for Pop. I've expressed my forgiveness to him several times. I wrote it to him and I wrote again to be sure that he knew I meant it and I wrote again to be sure that I meant it.

What do you wish your children to recall most about you? Your discipline, or your unconditional love? They need not be alive on this third dimension to know of either. They can view this from "up there."

Let me tell you who I am not. I am not my parents, but reflect from them what I do and do not wish to be. Everything I hate about me and everything I love reflects to me through them. Do you see where I'm going with this?

It's not the cop who writes you up or the parent who raises you. It's what they reflect to you. Often they reflect the person you will not own and if you won't claim ownership, you won't have power or authority to change that part of yourself.

I am not my first girlfriend who threatened suicide if I left her.

I am not my second girlfriend. A lady blessed with divine love for others.

I am not my third relationship that reflected lies as easily as truth.

I am not the one in the next relationship who, when drinking, would slap me across the face in a fit of rage if I wouldn't get out of bed for a chat.

There are many others who I am not, but I am the reflection of them and these mentioned. I could never know this until I stepped out of my own self-inflicted prison of self denial. All these people in my life, I as a soul, brought to me so that I could reflect the "who" I am and love to be and the "who" I am and hate to be. The correction of me is up to me.

Ditto the above for you in general. You, as a soul, draw precisely those people into your life who reflect you. YOU WILL DRAW WHOMEVER YOU ARE BEING! Reflect on this sentence. Contemplate it in silence for five minutes.

If you desire to find a soulmate of your favor, as so many of you do, then go back to the simple exercise I just gave you and do it. If you're down with the infamous dis-ease of, "It's a Saturday night and I ain't got nobody," even if the association, club, or bar is loaded with humans, think of this. If you're lonely and desire to fill that internal gap, does it make sense to you that by applying an external remedy (pick-up from wherever), you will succeed in fulfilling the internal lack? If the feeling of lack is emanating from within the heart, does it not make good, valid, common sense to go there to correct it rather than the "meet" house?

Everybody out here is a reflection of your internal condition. Don't wait for discord and dis-ease to summon you inward. Denial of daily emoting, expressing, and going within in quiet moments of meditation to your message from God center, the heart, creates the perception of separation of the body from the spirit and you from your desired mates. This imbalance is the cause of all dis-ease. The lack of emotional expressing diminishes the natural flow of energy on a cellular level resulting in, not only dis-ease, but aging. This also leads to suicidal tendencies.

If you would begin now to get in touch with the mighty "I AM" presence that is in the center of all of us, fully feeling your heart and allowing these feelings to flow outward, miracles would become a part of your life. By no means can you do this as long as you harbor judgment or denial. You must become alikened to the child.

Judgment blocks the rising of your life force up to the higher centers of the body. Another result of judgment. It brings your focus away from the creator of your life circumstances, YOU, and shifts it to the non-creator of your life circumstances, others—disconnecting you with your source of power. If you could realize that the behaviors you dislike in others are the same behaviors you are denying in yourself, how could you then direct judgment away from self? Every time you integrate a denied aspect of yourself, you give path to more true spirit and become more whole, "Whole 'I' Spirit." In this, you advance toward super consciousness.

An indicator that you have opened to suppressed emotions is finding yourself being bombarded by negativity, abuse, and destructive thoughts. You are then on the path of release. Do not step into the path of resistance, become like God; allow, observe and experience with integrity and ownership of your world in its full content. In the moments you have denied emotional energy to emote, energy in motion, you allowed guilt to take space that should have been filled with experience and understanding. Let not the guilt feeling fester into grief. When you are in grief, you are out of your personal power and guilt, too, is the reversal of power.

One good way to deny your feelings and assist others in denial of theirs is to play the role of the people pleaser/caretaker. This deprives others of taking responsibility for their own lives. In this role, you give excuses on behalf of others so they may continue to avoid answering to their own inner callings.

If your role for the day is being battered, you are repressing anger. The more guilt you embrace, the more abuse you draw. You must switch your attention away from the one causing the emotion to the emotion. Get into a habit of speaking up for yourself and you will not fall prey to this roleplay. You cannot look to the other person to solve your problems. They don't have your problems, you do. Oh, and by the way, if you happen to be the one who is doing the battering, have you ever heard the expression, "You will reap what you sow?"

In its full expression to buddy, buddette or butthead, whichever fits, wear that one. I did not let this part get edited out because I find it very helpful, in the uncovering of red buttons. So if you must judge it, so be it; but judgment in any form also comes in the muddy shade of red and is, in all cases, the drawing away from your true Christ self.

On bringing this chapter to its most important session, if you've not noticed, I'm the kinda guy that saves the good stuff for last. I would like to first give you my personal opinion, up to date, on that all-so-immensely-controversial-subject, SEX.

If one makes getting laid a goal, he is on a downhill losing struggle, with dis-ease, dis-agreement, dis-comfort, and disaster to become his future. This use of your vital energies leads to expedient aging and certain bodily destruction. You bind yourself by the earthly games you play to experience the effect of all their cause.

You need not be a biology major, scientist or theologian to ascertain, through a li'l good ol' common sense, that the sperm of the male and the blood of the female have within them the power to affect life into its creation.

When loveless sex is performed, power is spilled. When love toward the other is involved, power is increased. If you cannot love the one you're with, then get with the one you can. The song says, "Love the one you're with," not "Lay the one you're with." When you have sex without love, you are missing the true heartfelt joy intended in this divine activity. I say divine because, is this not the most powerful enjoyment of humans, to feel connectedness/oneness with the all? Will you have your sex with or without emotional attachment?

BENEFITS WITHOUT:
Relieving, aging, empty feelings, drained.

BENEFITS WITH:
Revitalizing, rejuvenating, refreshing, fulfilling,
fortifying, energizing, oneness.

When you can love the one you sex, you can roll over and say thank you for a lovely sharing in your temple; rather than, was it good for you? The more you are centered within yourself, the more fulfilling you will be for your partner. "To thine own self be centered."

Every problem we have, ever had, and ever will have is due to the turning of our attention away from our own personal mighty, "I AM" presence. Have you ever thanked God for the experiencing of an orgasm? This is one of, if not the most Godly things one can experience in this dimension. The more you give attention to, thanks for, and use your mighty "I AM" presence, the more quickly it will begin to respond to you. You must maintain peace and harmony for the divine presence to expand its perfection and healing into your outer activities, to include the attracting of your divine partners.

I wish that you have life abundantly and if your wish is congruent with mine, then place not one condition on another human being ever again and your wish can come true.

Unconditional awareness is a simple repenting, changing of the mind. By relinquishing, from your personality, the setting of conditions on others you are not losing control of yourself or your life. You are allowing others the same thing that God allows us all, FREE WILL. Now if you happen to think yourself smarter than your creator, you may not get the gest of this. Keep it real simple; "If binding don't work, loose it." If the way you've been livin' ain't workin', try another way.

PS. For you western (hemispherically speaking) stud-muffins: *The study of Taoist or Tantric Sex can change your life forever.*

A SPECIAL NOTE TO THE MALE AND FEMALE SPECIES INHABITING THIS PLANET:

Through the act of sexual exchange, there is awesome healing and regenerating power... OR, through the continual loss of semen (more especially the male seed through ejaculation), ill health and degeneration are eminent. Eyesight weakens, hair loss, loss of stamina, inability to concentrate, rapid aging, etc. However, through proper use and channeling of this powerful natural energy, you may bring yourself to unbelievable health, vitality, and miraculous union in your relationships.

With continued upward focusing on the higher centers of the body through the sexual experiencing of each other, you may bring yourself to enlightenment.

I recommend the readings of Sunyata Saraswati and Bodhi Avinasha *Jewel in The Lotus*, and Mantak Chia's writings on this subject.

We will go much further into the truths of the awesome transforming powers of sex in the second book. I will use space now to say that the methods of properly transmuting our own God powers through this wonderful medium have been almost completely hidden from, lost by, not passed on, locked up, forgotten, overlooked, unused, and/or, misunderstood by them, us, and their forefathers. Sex has been exploited as something dangerous, nasty, dirty, evil, and even unnatural to such a tremendous degree that to mention it in the workplace could get you in the courtroom.

I now always include God and meditation in all my earthly activities, most especially this one.

CHAPTER 18

How to Pray

"If you come to me with doubt
I will give you every reason to be doubtful.
If you come to me with love,
I will show you more than you have ever known."

-Mahamuni Babaji

"From the Almighty I Am Presence, I call forth clarity, I step aside, you lead the way." In case you're not sure of what you need, want, or desire, this affirmation will assist in clearing up that disorder. You might start your prayer by saying, "Father (Source), what should I pray for? Show me what I need to know."

Reawaken to the basics and get fixed on using them as often as needed, "Ask and ye shall receive," but for the sake of clarity, ask clear questions. If you are not in the activity of verbally or mentally asking Universe clear questions, how could She be giving clear answers to you? BE DEFINITE WITH THE INFINITE!

The Father of Quantum Physics, Mr. Heidelberg, put it thusly, "The universe does not reveal its secrets, but responds to a method of questioning."

Who ya' gonna' call? God? Who's that? Where's She live?

Why call on someone or thing you don't know? Well you do know!

You just forgot! Listen closely, you may befriend an old runnin' buddy/ buddette. This is where the secret ingredient comes in.

God came here to earth, in a fully conscious way back in the year Zero by means of His only begotten son, Jesus, right? Now let not this word beguile you. I took the liberty to look it up, the word "begotten" that is. You must go to the fathering word, beget, in the dictionary, which means to create or cause. The word begotten is not only referred to in biblical teaching in the four references to the "only begotten son," but a total of twenty-four times throughout the Bible or what's left of it, King Jim boy edition. Deep study? Indeed! You will discover the most common meaning of the word begotten from the biblical interpretations: the bringing forth from one's self, a person, thing, or circumstance.

Many believe that Mary, mother of Jesus, was not blessed with that nasty, dirty, sinful, God-given opportunity to enjoy the sexual experience in the bringing forth of this particular child. Rather than dispute it, stimulating the need-to-be-right syndrome within you, know that a seed is a seed and a cell is a cell and there be but one who manifests them all and that be the ALL. That is, no matter how you arrived, you came from the one and only giver of life, the All That Is; therefore, you too are divine.

I express this for an extremely important reason. Believe it or not, there are walking, talking, breathing human beings on this planet today who believe Jesus is the only qualified being who can be or is begotten of God. Of course, these entities of whom I speak will thump John 1:14, 1:18, 3:16 and 3:18 and say, "SEE RIGHT HERE, IT'S IN THE BOOK."

Kinda' slam-dunk feeling, you're the ball, and after they cool down a bit from the "want-to-be-right syndrome," will they then extend with that awesome, open-minded display of their way of seeking truth, the other twenty expressions of the meaning of begotten? Then, in this almighty book of more paradoxical controversies than any I have ever studied, will they go on to explain, or try to understand John 16:15 that states, "All things that the Father hath are mine." As they get stumped, they just say, "Well you got to read the whole book." So I did. They never seemed to dwell much on these most powerful statements.

Not only did the master Jesus state, "All these things I have done, so shall ye do." "Ye are all of the most high." If you believe in the basic gist of the Bible as I do, those statements, among many other direct and powerful statements made by Jesus were not made by just sonny boy who got booted down here to undergo that unpleasant job he accepted to do. They were produced, directed and issued forth by God Himself, were they not? "The Father and I are one." "If you have seen me, you have seen Source." Get this part through your beanie cap and you will begin to perceive the unconventional idea that God is an indoor kinda' guy!

If these targeted words got your dander up, it's not the God in you that's riled, He doesn't get that way. It's just altered ego. You know that little guy with horns who has kept you here till now! Obviously, here is where you are. Can you think of someone else to cast your blame or poor-me-victim syndrome toward. You see, there is only one God (Universal Source). The illusion of a second God is in the turning away from the "Presence."

God knew then as now, we were gettin' into the muck of fear because of our lack in faith; so He, a part of His higher consciousness, descended, for easy reference, through means of a highly evolved part of himself, Jesus, in fourth density, so as to show us how to regain our footing on the path, as it were. He knew how we could just give up trying when we don't see, hear, smell, taste, or feel His power. So He reintroduced us to the key ingredient necessary for our time, FAITH—that which will open your higher senses to the power of the God "I AM" within us all.

It is alleged that we, our governments, asked some ET's who God is. Their answer, "The Universe!"

One thing to keep in mind, this source is always pressing out from within, always asking, "WHAT DO YOU WANT?" and if you are not giving your own answers, doing your own thinking, then I've got news for ya'! The problem here is the basic nature of the common thoughts circulating upon this gorgeous planet. Lack, want, limitation, fear, guilt, shame and lo-o-o-w self esteem, etc.

Rent "Ghost Busters." The green slime is the human discordant thoughts.

There is a power that holds this universe on course. They say this power animates, penetrates, and motivates the entire cosmos. In defining the activity of this power, instead of the name, there are two sources we can go to; science or theology.

The word science means, "to know" or organized knowledge. Science will say: there is an energy that just is. It is neither created nor destroyed. It is the cause and effect of itself and is 100% present in all places at all times.

Theologians will say: there is a power in the cosmos we call God, he just is. He is neither created nor destroyed. He is the cause and effect of himself. He is 100% present in all places at all times, omnipresent.

The only difference here is the name. Science is studying the energy around humanity. Theology is studying the energy within humanity. Eventually they will discover that they are studying the same force.

Know that this power source is always ready for you to apply it.

HOW NOT TO PRAY

When you go to the restaurant to dine out, do you beg for the food there? Do you serve it? Do you cook it? Command to the universal supply house, knowing that you will receive. "Command Ye Me." Giving thanks to God in advance for the thing or condition desired is alikened unto giving gratuity in advance to the Maitre d' to assure good service and seating. Don't beg God. Thank Him in advance. This will keep the latitude of your attitude in gratitude.

Never begin, continue, or end prayers by calling yourself negative names like, "Lord we are unworthy" and how dare you speak in such tones on behalf of the group? If you feel the need to call yourself sinner, shameful, unworthy, etc., then at least have the common courtesy not to condemn others at the gathering to that level of low vibration. Keep it personal, thank you.

When you pray for another in a hospital bed in a bad way, don't envision them as such. Let your visions carry health, wealth, and joy. Send love and light, let God place it. Your prayers do have power either way you use them. Know this, the universe *always* works in a circular motion. The prayer sent out will, of like manner, return to its sender magnified. I will now share an enlightening experience in how a well meant prayer boomeranged to the sender.

One Monday morning, living in Salina, Kansas, I awoke in a most unusual state of emotion; anxiety, depression, emptiness, and some of their relatives. A proper two-word description for how I felt may be termed psychic attack. Initially, I had no idea what was going on inside me. It was not like me to miss work. However, this was so intense that I could not go to work.

Periodically through the day, this powerful, negative energy continued to return. My "feelings" were in the grinder, my emotional body was kickin' the fickle material outta' me. What in hell was going on?

That evening finally came, thank God! I could now just sleep it away, so I thought. I tossed and turned until finally I did thank God and had a short talk with His boy, then fell off to sleep.

The next morning arrived. I woke up feeling just as bad as I felt yesterday. No work today! Something seriously wrong needed a fix. I skipped breakfast, got out my books and began to read and review some of the ol' Harold Sherman and Joseph Weed Rosicrucian Teachings on meditations and psychic powers. I read and meditated all day.

Later that evening something came to mind that I hadn't done in some time. So I sat and stilled my mind and began to recite an ol' prayer by Mary Wood, a great teacher who lived in, believe it or else, Peculiar, Missouri.

The prayer, mantra, or request is as follows: "Beloved Father surround me in the great white Light of Christ so all that is good may enter and all else must return to whence it came." I must have repeated this fifty times up till bedtime, then I lay down and repeated, "Jesus Christ" over and over till I fell asleep.

I awoke Wednesday morning feeling refreshed, revitalized, and emotionally intact. The condition was literally gone. I fixed breakfast and prepared for a get-out-there-and-sell, sell, sell makeup kinda' workday. Then the phone rang. Before I enlighten you on who called, allow me to explain the experience of the preceding weekend.

I had driven to Kansas City where my parents lived. On Sunday afternoon I went out to a buffet with Mom and Dad as they returned from church with their dear ol' friends, Kirt and Marcile.

On the drive back from lunch, my father and I were beginning to communicate somewhat confrontationally, as in our past discussions about religion and spiritual beliefs. You see, I was a no-show for church that morning. Are you up with me so far? Now as I may be in the act of passing judgment here, let me express my now perception of Daddy.

Never will you meet a more honest human being. His integrity is impeccable. His magnanimity unmatchable. His endurance, thirty six years at Armco Steel. A heart of gold, a body of twisted steel, "IRONMAN." I don't know if anyone could whoop my daddy cause no one ever attempted the job. I heard a story though, that once, when I was knee-high to a grasshopper, three guys came into our yard in Kansas City. You know the song, "Going to Kansas City," the part that refers to 19th and Vine. We lived there and we're not talkin' Beverly Hills, if you know what I mean. Anyway, I heard that my daddy removed the "gentleman" who came through our gate, over the fence. Now let me ask you, if you were child to "that," would you ever "talk back?" I somehow never required the first experience to know better. Now you have a briefing on who I used to argue religion with.

The altercations never began until I had the courage to face the "lion's den," "Ironman," and only after Vietnam, several types of martial arts schools, sparring with pro-boxers and wrestling a 750 pound bear. After Victor the bear, I was ready to discuss any topic with Pop, even though I did not pin Victor.

Well, as Kirt was driving and Dad was a front seat passenger, I was strategically positioned between the ladies in the back seat. During the chat, I discovered that Dad had learned I was doing some kinda "fortune telling" and rumor had it that I may even have a crystal ball. Now understand, my father, to my knowledge, has never been accused of being "open minded" but is, let's say stationary in his orthodox, Southern Baptist belief system, and in the book of his faith, the Bible. If you don't follow the correct procedure to get to heaven, you don't go, but you go to the everlasting pit of fire and brimstone. Like the human brothers who taught him that particular way of thinking, they scare the hell out of you to get you to heaven because "it's my job." He seems to express more emphasis on the hell part than the heaven part.

At my father's instructions, many, times, "READ THE BOOK, READ THE BOOK." So I read the book.

It is quite interesting and quite controversial, and also leaves you "quite hanging," in that, I would go over the chapters, over and over, and compare and still have the similar questions of, "Which way did this writer mean that this time?"

There is scripture that speaks of "the fortune tellers" in the final days. As Dad was chiding me about fortune telling, I leaned a little closer and said, "but Dad, anyone can tell his future and I'll tell you how."

WHOA!, OH NO!" Dad shouted. Dad got hot and loud.

Just in time, Kirt, also 30 years plus at Armco and a li'l larger than Dad, came to my rescue with a louder, "ALVIN, LISTEN TO YOUR SON!" I resubmitted, "the way, in which anyone can tell their future, is by simply looking at his now."

If you are reacting today, you will be reacting tomorrow because you gave birth and sustained it by feeding it what it lives on. If you are a responder today, you will be a responder tomorrow. You may live life as does Captain Kirk or Spock. The choice is yours.

Did the master Jesus not say, "Peace be still"? Is it not written, if you wish to know God, you must "Be Still."

At this point, our conversation went to football. Dad had to cool down after that good sense psychology.

Daddy, if I complete this book before you find yourself in that sweet by-and-by, know that I know you gave me all you had to give and that I love you for it and thank you for it.

Now, about that Wednesday morning phone call. It was Sis, she said, "David, I thought I had better call you and let you know that Dad is in the hospital."

Let me add here, my dad is one of those kinda' guys that don't go to hospitals. Mama always used to say, "He'll outlive me by a long shot."

That did come to pass, as Mama left this plane in her mid-70's. Dad is headed for triple digit, so it seems.

I apologize for the detailed story, but you must know how not to pray, as well as how to. When Mama spoke the aforementioned statement, "Dad will outlive me," that's a prayer. The universe is always listening.

When Dad, in his powerful prayers, prayed for me that God would go, get the devil out of Billy (my middle name), I'm thinking he had more a fixation on evil than good. Whatever you send out returns, and if you send it directly and the entity to whom you intend it towards is surrounded in light, it returns directly.

My personal conviction is that no evil, even well intended, will be at a level of vibration to penetrate "THE LIGHT OF CHRIST" not in its own solar system. When you take it upon yourself to pray for another, I admonish you, don't send any prayers, thoughts, ideas, or intents that you wouldn't want to live with. Send love and light. It knows what to do from there. Light saves, you don't! Ten thousand of you cannot save one other but one of us, as an illuminated example, can save ten thousand, or at least lead them toward it.

At this point, let me admonish you on the asking for things like patience. If you require or would like to have the quality of being patient, don't ask the universe for patience, be patient. The universe knows all the qualifying activities that may cause one to become patient and will send you as much of them as you beg for.

For example, if you ask for patience, you may find yourself on the freeway behind a long line of traffic awaiting the removal of a turned over vehicle, or in a long line at the grocery store and when it's finally your turn, the cashier runs out of change. Still not accepting what you ask for, you go for your checkbook so that you won't need to wait for change. You write your check to the wrong store or you fill in the wrong amount. You tear out the check and realize it was your last, so you continue to wait. Not patient yet? The clerk finishes and then the sacker drops the only thing you really needed anyway, the eggs. He runs back to get more, as you continue to wait, but they're out. It begins to rain, you get everything home, including the ice cream. Lightening hits the local transformer and the lights go out, no electricity. Now what? Are you patient yet? If you desire patience, don't ask, but be patient.

The Lord's Prayer is an excellent prayer that intends gratitude, which is the best attitude. However, you should say it not in vain, ritualistic repetition, but put meaning into it to empower you. Now to know a more proper translation of its meaning. Let me share?

OUR (collectively belonging to all)

FATHER (the source of all for all)

WHO IS IN HEAVEN (most high mind)

HALLOWED (sacred, revered)

BE THY NAME (your individual Christian name or first name).

THY KINGDOM (the realm in which God's will is fulfilled)

COME (be revealed unto you consciously)

THY WILL (souls divine plan)

BE DONE, ON EARTH (outer personality)

AS IN HEAVEN (your divine mind).

PROVIDE US DAILY OUR NEEDED BREAD
(spiritual nourishment).

FORGIVE (cancel out)

US OF OUR WRONGS AS WE FORGIVE WRONGS. LET US YIELD NOT TO TEMPTATION, BUT DELIVER US FROM EVIL (Living toward third dimension desires rather than from divine inner guidance).

FOR THINE IS THE TRUE KINGDOM AND THE POWER (animator of all life and energy source)

AND THE GLORY
(magnificence, eternity, state of great exaltation)

FOREVER (limitless time).

AUM (A-Creator God I AM, U-Preserver God I AM, M-Transformer God I AM)

You may have a difference of opinion about how the original "Lord's Prayer" was worded. One example may be the sentence, "Let us yield not to temptation." It could be versed, "Leave us not in temptation." But it never was originated with the familiar, "Lead us not." God does not lead us into temptation. Would you lead your children toward evil? Are you gettin' the idea that it's just downright possible you've been misled even through "their" translations of the bible?

SHOULD WE PRAY FOR SOMETHING LIKE MONEY?

Personally I have nothing against that green stuff said to answer all things: Ecclesiastics 10:19.

However, have you looked up the word "thing." I have. It basically represents inanimate material objects. So, it hasn't anything in the world to do with anything; let's say, above it. Except maybe its symbolic representation of what comes to you from your efforts, seeds sown, of creative, or specified output. If one asks, believing to receive, it is a done deal. So where's my million bucks I prayed for last night? If you truly believed you would be creating, doing what brings about a million bucks—product, service, or idea, any of these can be worth a million to someone. You are, in fact, a co-creating God with the manifesting God-head of you. If you quit creating, the God-head of you is disconnected to your avenue of expression; no expression... no experience; no experience... no growth; no growth... no harvest; no harvest... no million bucks. You do not have to create your life, it can all be done for you. However, if you are not intentionally, deliberately creating your own life on purpose—your purpose—it shouldn't be a very purposeful life experience.

Back to the drawing (expressing) board. Pray for the memory of who you are. Ask the beloved Father to reveal Christ, His perfect son, unto you. Then bless the "I AM Christ of you" and know that you know He already has! You are within the Source and the Source is within you.

Does the apple tree pray for apples? Remember God is an indoor kinda' guy. He is always out-pressing. You are always allowing or damning. The choice is in your freewill.

Remember Source communicated the fact, "I will supply all your needs." The thing about being in a freewill type of environment is, you have the automatic right to be, have or do. To circumvent or override this environmental-type condition that allows one the, let's say, availability for vacation away from home, kingdom. You must inform the universe of your intent or desire.

It's a most helpful key to keep in mind as you ask, seek, and knock for your desires to manifest from Source, that you know you are not separate, but through chain of command, just "down line."

Seek ye first to reunite in consciousness with creation itself. The more you do unite in awareness with creation, all of it, the more you realize you are Creator of your own life, all of it.

Universe sends its energies to the ones using the most of it; creating, expressing, loving, and experiencing it. Holy Spirit, guides, angels, etc., are availed to those who create a momentum. "To those who hath it shall be added."

Here's a down home kinda' (perception clearing) story:

Billy and Johnny were average little males species, trouble makers, as they were growing up. They would go around town gettin' in trouble and if they didn't do it, they got the blame anyway. Just their kinda' luck, ya' know?

Well, as they were out gettin' in trouble, and gettin' the blame when they weren't, their mother got a loud knock at the front door from her neighbor. As she opened the door, he was obviously upset. He held a baseball in her face screaming, "Those little brats of yours broke my window and you're gonna' pay."

She asked, "Did you see them commit this terrible crime?"

He replied, "NO!, but who else is always in trouble around here?

Now are you gonna' pay for my window or will it be Small Claims Court to help you make up your mind?"

Well, now Mama was all upset. She just couldn't understand why her boys always got the blame for everything. She got on the phone and called the church she occasionally visited. The pastor answered the call.

"Hello Reverend, I know I haven't been coming to church regularly, but I was hoping you could at least give me some advice in a family matter. You see, my husband left about six years ago and I have been trying my best to raise Billy and Johnny on my own. They just keep gettin' in trouble and even stuff that they don't do, they get the blame for. Now I'm gonna' have to come up with more money to pay for something I don't think they did at all, or go to court with my neighbor over the matter. I just don't know who to…"

"Ma'am!, please just calm down now, I'll be glad to help you. Bring Billy and Johnny on down here to me."

As Mama walked into the pastor's office, she's just going on and on, "Here they are, running around gettin' in trouble, gettin' the blame when they're not guilty. I just don't know what to do with 'em."

"PLEASE! Hon, you just let me take care of Billy and Johnny. You go on home and I'll drop 'em off when I GET DONE WITH 'EM, okay?

"All right Billy, you wait over here across the hall in this room. JOHNNY, YOU COME TO MY OFFICE! Sit down here! Now, Johnny I'm gonna' ask you some questions AND I WANT SOME ANSWERS!"

The pastor looked at Johnny and asked, "Now Johnny, first I want to know, WHERE'S GOD?"

Johnny, with a look of surprise, glared into the eyes of the pastor, with no reply.

"JOHNNY, I asked you a question, WHERE IS GOD?"

Johnny began to sweat and turn different colors in the face as his heart beat faster and faster, his blood seemed to boil.

The pastor stared Johnny down and said loudly, "JOHNNY, I'm only gonna' ask you one last time, WHERE'S GOD?"

JOHNNY JUMPED UP OUT OF THE CHAIR, RAN DOWN THE HALL, GRABBED BILLY AND SAID, "COME ON BILLY, WE GOTTA' GET OUTTA' HERE. GOD'S MISSING AND WE'RE GONNA' GET THE BLAME FOR IT!"

Now let me ask you...

Have you ever felt like God is missing in your life? Well, if so, guess who moved?

From my profound personal experience, I will share with you what made the difference for me and what has brought me to a new plateau of observership. There is a title for this li'l poem that explains this difference in my life, it's called:

THE DIFFERENCE

I got up early one morning
    and rushed right into the day.

I had so much to accomplish
    that I didn't have time to pray.

Problems just tumbled about me,
    heavier came each task.

Why doesn't God help me? I wondered,
    He answered, you didn't ask!"

I wanted to see joy and beauty,
    but the day toiled on gray and bleak.

I wondered why God didn't show me,
    He said, "but you didn't seek."

I tried to come into God's presence
    I used all my keys at the lock.

God gently and lovingly told me,
    "my child, you didn't knock."

I woke up early this morning,
    and paused before entering the day.

I had so much to accomplish,
    that I decided to take time to pray.

PRAYERS

Often as I arise is the morning, I begin it with something like this:

"Beloved Father within, I now humbly ask that you take over my affairs for this day. Guide me to say and do the right things all day.

"I have faith in the Father within, and now place myself in the divine center of all good and constructive action. Knowing only good can come to me, I am now in the center of divine action, and everything I say and do will be prompted by the higher divine word within me."

AND / OR

"I choose joy for every experience in this day."

AND / OR

"Make every step I take today bring me one step closer to you."

AND / OR

"Beloved Almighty, I am present. Thank you for this day, this home, this bed. Guide me today. Show me where I need to go, what I need to know, and connect me with those whom I need to meet."

Just as Jesus did, you too may go direct to the Source. Jesus said, "I go unto my Father."

Jesus showed us then how to bring the Christ activity of God, Source, Monadic Essence, Creation, Spirit, call it what you may, but call on it. Do it in the quietude of your heart and mind and stay in touch daily. Watch your life as the observer, see how it gradually unfolds and blossoms into life more abundant than you ever dreamed possible.

You can go to the ocean with a teaspoon or a bucket, the ocean doesn't care, or you can pipe in through daily affirmations, prayer and meditation. You are not taking from anyone. You are receiving, to the level of your acceptance, from the LIMITLESS SOURCE. Know that God is the one experiencing life by means of you.

If you are confused, and in our time of educated denial, confusion is more common than weeds, ask God what He would like to experience through you today! "Beloved Father, what is your will? Let thy will be mine. Show me, over the next several days, what you would like to experience through my body." Then become calm and serene, so as to receive the messages and messengers. They will come.

Give thanks, no matter how good or bad the things that begin to tumble down or build up around you are. If one wishes to build a new HOUSE where the old one sits, the old must go. LET IT! God knows if you need new surroundings, home, mate, car, or job. Let go and let God, your super mind, soul in you, guide you.

To benefit the scientific minded, I'll express some of the more specific facts of your manifesting power source.

We've been educated on different ways the earth was created. Well, pick your favorite, I don't convert, I share. We do, however, have good, solid, three-dimensional evidence of Her existence. So how does She remain suspended, if I may for easy reference use that word, in mid-space, gravity pull, energy fields, etc. from or to other planets, sun, stars or the energy fields from without or within Her?

Personally, if I never know during this trip, I won't feel I missed out. However, what I find most interesting is that ol' statement, "BY MY WORD THIS ALL EXISTS."

Please note for term reference, the key word here is "WORD." Science says it takes twenty-six muscle groups or seventy-two different muscles to produce one word. As the word comes verbally through your voice, it literally creates horsepower that propels, thrusts, motivates, etc.

The human voice, transformed into electrical energy for wireless transmission, develops 270 horsepower. In a sense of energy variations, you could say words, along with what you place before or behind them, cause their energy vibrational effect on the sender as well as the receiver, to a degree.

Let's say that you took a couple of the most common words of the English vocabulary, like, "I can't," and whatever topic you follow them with, would add to the effect. Just to get the gist here, let's multiply.

I CAN'T (2 words) Good, now let's be sparing and say one uses this term one hundred and fifty times per week, for one year.

2 words x 270 h.p. = 540 h.p.
540 h.p. x 150 times= 81,000 h.p.
81,000 h.p. x 52 weeks = 4,212,000 h.p.

I can't make ends meet, pass the test, afford a new_____.

You have three ways in which to create life, your life. Your words are one. With them, you can create, dis-create or re-create your life. They are indeed a power source of flowing energy.

You may acquire your own proof easily by placing your attention and becoming aware of the general vocabulary of your family members, friends, and others you hear. You will note quite different vocabularies between the happy and unhappy individual, the peaceful or hostile, healthy or sick, wealthy or struggler.

Your words, actions, and thoughts are your three sources of creation and when you change any one of these three, the other two will follow.

You are created in the image of the Creator. That is why you have a speaker on your face, and if through it, words that create come out, you create. If words to block, damn, un-create, dis-create, resist, damage, or deny utter out, that will be the effect. If you're not sure what to say in a situation or conversation, don't say! Plead the fifth or just walk around saying, "I AM." Just be sure to follow these words with what you prefer to be "I AM" ?????

I'd say about 99% of all people's prayers are simply the words spoken in their waking hours; which by the way, overrides that two hours a week many spend so faithfully going to church by about one hundred sixty six hours to two.

If you know someone who recites a phrase like, "I can't make ends meet," I'll just bet you a dollar to a doughnut, that they are pretty darn close to exemplification of that statement in their life.

Imagine when the bills keep on piling up you walk around reciting, "I AM ends meet."

The only humans who are starving to death are the souls that chose that particular method of experience for their personal, divine plan. I didn't say don't help them; give 'em your shirt and shoes. Don't empower that condition with words like, "that poor soul." They are not poor souls, they all came from limitless Source. There is a plan for each, by each. If you truly desire to assist them, teach them the same as the great masters taught us. Give a man a fish, he can only eat for a day. Teach them, by becoming the example of ample, by accepting more abundance for yourself. "Above all things I wisheth that you prosper, earn, and circulate lots of greenback, have abundance, and possess the land, buy real estate. What I'm pressing on you here is to be sure you have shirt and shoes. "To thine own Self, be centered."

We have spoken to you of the three ways you have to create. Your thoughts, words and actions. These are your creating powers and you use them all day long.

The most important realization you can come to about these energies is the source of energy that propels them out, and how they cause the circumstances to appear in your living space.

NUMBER 1: The motivator of these... YOUR FEELINGS.
Your feelings provide four to seven times more energy than the thought they charge. Express your feelings in your intent or desire.

NUMBER 2: The director of these is your attention. Whatever you allow your thoughts to drift upon, becomes your circumstances. Set your focus of attention on *only that which you prefer to have, see, experience, or become.*

We have enlightened you with mantras and prayers. Keep it simple, use the ones that resonate to you, that you feel comfortable with. Apply some of the following mantras. Intone them three, six, or twelve times. What matters most is that you practice some form of prayer. As you become more familiar with your favorite practice, intone them softly but firmly, smoothly, and with more and more perfection. It's not the mantra you are perfecting. God has already taken care of that. It is the performer that you are tuning up, YOU.

The power is in the director, YOU. If someone else performs the mantra for you, what good could it do for you? The mantras empower you, yes, but not until you do them. This intends your acceptance of the universal vibration of the God source.

Intone the mantra and speak the affirmation with the heart-felt energies of COMMAND and DEMAND in your consciousness until your words become your feelings turned inside out.

∽ ∽ ∽ ∽ ∽ ∽ ∽ ∽ ∽ ∽ ∽ ∽ ∽ ∽

MANTRAS

∽ ∽ ∽ ∽ ∽ ∽ ∽ ∽ ∽ ∽ ∽ ∽ ∽ ∽

"I Am the outer expression of the mighty
I AM Presence, God."

"I AM focused on God's direction.
Reveal to me your divine plan."

"I AM the presence of perfection
experiencing life of God in man."

"I AM the resurrection and the life."

"Beloved, Almighty, most high, living God.
    Surround me in, around and through
    with your great white pillar of protective light,
    All powerful, impenetrable, divine light,
    so all that is good and necessary
    may enter and all, not of this light,
    may not enter.

Let thy will be mine.
Let our will combine.
Let thy will be done.
Let our will be one."

End your prayers and meditations with something like this:

"I AM a child of the light.

I love the light.

I serve the light.

I live in the light.

I AM protected, illumed, supplied,
    and sustained by the light.
    I bless the light.

I AM the light.

I AM the light.

I AM, I AM, I AM."

I'll leave you with one additional thought to ponder at the close of this chapter. Choose one: "I CAN'T" or "I AM." They are both a prayer.

When you speak, know this. You are in the activity of manipulating light into energy with thought. The energy activated by your words has no choice but to manifest the product, idea, or activity of its intent or nature if continually expressed, through verbiage, action, or thought. All of the ALL is within the two words, "I AM."

We take our ability to speak for granted so much. When was the last time you paused for a minute (minute pause) and said, "Thank you Father for giving me a voice for communication?"

Stay fixed in the attitude of gratitude, mentally, emotionally, and verbally.

Begin your day with inductions of the force that beats your heart.

Beloved Almighty "I AM" Presence, make every step
I take today bring me one step closer to you.

"God is seeking you and if you move one step closer to God,
God moves one-hundred steps closer to you."
–Sathya Sai Baba

A Powerful Song

I am the Light, I am the Love,
I am the Glory from God above.
Auhhh-h-h-h-h-h-h

I am the Love, I am the Light,
I am the Glory that shines through the night.
Ohm-m-m-m-m-m-m

Focus: On the meaning in the words and then on
the mantra.

Effect: manifestation.

> *"I AM the commanding presence,*
> *the exhaustless energy and the divine*
> *wisdom causing my desire to be fulfilled."*

Thank you for reading the words "I AM" writing.
Now let me introduce you to another power of yours.

CHAPTER 19

The Power In Meditation

"All of man's troubles stem from his inability to sit quietly in a room alone."

-Blaise Pascal

BENEFITS OF MEDITATION

Slowly and naturally a measure of control of the mind emerges. You begin to sense the truth more clearly, gaining greater compassion for others. Simply being still causes expansion of awareness, improves understanding, perception, and allows emotional detachment; heightens your senses, reduces stress, and improves health, bringing peace, centeredness, self-discipline and a greater ability to focus.

Visual imagery increases in conscious receptivity.

Regeneration of the physical, mental, emotional, and etheric bodies alters the process of aging. Note: The emotional body receives rest only during the conscious stilling of the mind. You are no exception to this rule.

Quickening of your psychic gifts leading to development of a new and subtle apparatus, by means of which you no longer see the vision of divine reality as separate, but know yourself to be divine reality, and finally leads to illumination and inspiration.

Please keep this simple, all you need do is learn to concentrate just a little today, each day. That's all, everything else will fall into place. The word, CONCENTRATION, in Latin is:

CON = Together or bring together

CENTRATE/centrare = Draw to a common center or focal point, or to center.

PROCESS OF MEDITATION

Your intent shapes light immediately. The reflection of memory equates likened to kinetic energy and gives way unto centrifugal force, what is called power or energy. Intelligence is in the thought. Thought is called electrical current. The power is in the thought. Your will is the power, your feelings are the energizer, your attention is director.

Changing thought does not require effort, only awareness and attention. Thomas Edison said, "Any thoughts, plans, goals, or ideas continually thought upon, in the conscious mind, must come into existence from the supernatural world."

It has also been stated, "The light of the body is the eye. If, therefore, thine eye be single, thy whole body shall be full of light."

Between the intellect and the intuition a gap exists until it has been consciously bridged through meditation. Meditation is sometimes defined as "thinking in the heart." Correct meditation proceeds only when the heart and mind function together in unison. To touch the intuition, therefore, this blending of heart and mind is a necessity.

Right use of the mind in meditation opens the consciousness to the beauty, truth and goodness of the soul through the five stages; concentration, meditation, contemplation, illumination, and inspiration. These five stages lead to union with the soul, "the son of mind," and direct knowledge of divinity, creating an instrument of intelligence for the soul to use in daily life.

In the early stages of meditation, the aspirant will notice a sense of loss, lack, and emptiness which is frequently most distressing. This is due to the fact that the focus of attention is away from the things of the senses. This indicates a certain sign of genuine progress in your mediations.

One of the first effects of the meditation work is usually an increased efficiency in the daily life; be it home, office or any field of human endeavor. Whether illumination is achieved or not through the practice of concentration and meditation, the life of the individual will be greatly enriched. There will be much gained power and awareness.

To excel in meditation the student should obtain the attitude of the observer in daily life, the onlooker or perceiver. Keep in mind here that observation draws to the observer what is being observed. We are not teaching you to focus on negativities. Turn your cheek toward what you do prefer.

Imagine yourself to be the thinker, unaffected by the feeling center in any negative way. Steadily guiding the thoughts received, refusing to allow unwanted thoughts to take root in our mind, not by inhibiting or resisting, but by the method of a dynamic interest in something else.

To assist growth, maintain close attention to your daily activities; whether reading a book, speaking with someone, driving a vehicle, cleaning the home, performing office or employment duties—whatever the activity of the moment. True ability to concentrate grows out of a concentrated thought-governed life.

Organize your daily life, regulate your activities. Become focused and one-pointed in your manner of living. Don't let your feelings push you, but guide you. People who are governed by their emotions waste much time and energy, and accomplish less than the mentally focused person.

There are at least six trillion reasons to still the body and mind and go within. Your body is made up of six trillion cells and it believes everything you tell it or impress upon it. There is a cosmic law that your body is in continual change. Whether you are adding to, subtracting from, or not doing anything at all, your cells are regenerating toward love, fear, or one of their relatives in between at a rate of ten million cells per second. If you are not doing the thinking, intending, or programming for this changing process, it's being done for you by the world's thinking, which by the way is, as it always has been, the wider case.

All levels of our mind can be controlled and addressed through meditation. It is this simple exercise that puts us on the road to controlling the communication of all levels of our mind.

Your mind, like your physical body, is also one of your vehicles of expression, "the mind-body." So your awareness may now expand when I say, "you," or "your," I am referring to you, the first person, SPIRIT; the perfect, unblemished director of your life. Each time you give way to the divine mind, that is the true YOU within. "Draw nigh unto me." "Let that mind be in you." You begin the process to REMEMBER WHO YOU ARE!

Is it seeping through? Are you having questions enter your mind at a rapid rate as you ponder this scripture?

Do the Ma-Na Mantra and it'll seep in. Simply sit and repeat ma-na, ma-na, ma-na for five minutes a day for a week and then observe the new memory activation in you.

For the I AM PRESENCE to come, you must clear the mind. To clear the mind, you must befriend the li'l bugger with gentle persuasion. As thoughts crowd up onto the heels of your mind, ask they be gone, simple as that. A fast mind is sick. By no means am I saying close any parts of the mind here. A closed mind has no room for growth. A slow mind is sound. A still mind is divine.

Before beginning my meditations, I sit, sometimes lotus style, legs crossed on the floor; sometimes in a comfortable chair, legs not crossed, hands on lap, palms up, first finger and thumb of each hand touching, forming a circle. I always begin with some form of deep breathing; conscious, rhythmic, diaphragmatic, deep smooth breaths.

If you would choose to accept but one activity of health improvement for any reason, and I'm talkin' holistically here, choose to sit for five to ten of your precious earth minutes each day and breathe deeply and smoothly, for at least 2-3 minutes.

Everyone has a pretty good idea about negative reaction and what it does to the human carcass, and that may be a most appropriate title for something that is treated with hurry, worry, fear, guilt, shame, the unworthy attitude, anger, remorse, resentment, jealousy, revenge, and stuffed full with some of the most unnecessary substances for reenergizing it.

Science has discovered that by surrounding the human being with positive emotions only, it seems not to age and suggests that if you would do that for the entire life of the person, this person would live to an incredulous and incredible old age.

Do you know science research on breathing of the air? Well, I reckon I'll just go ahead on and tell ya' cause I looked it up.

BREATH AND THE LYMPHATIC SYSTEM

Lymphatic System: see Lymph, Lymph cell, Lymph gland.

Your entire body is only as healthy as the cells that make it up. What determines how healthy your cells are is the bloodstream, where every cell must grow and live. If the cells are maintained they will be strong. If the cells are polluted too much, for too long, they cause the carrier to become weak, lose energy, and die if not corrected.

Air cleans the circulatory system. Breath is the foundation of all life on this planet. Breath gives cells what they need to live—oxygen. Breathing controls the flow of Lymph fluid to your body.

Lymph fluid contains white blood cells that protect your entire body and cleanse the system. The Lymph system has been referred to as the body's waste system. Every cell in your body is surrounded by Lymph. You have four times more Lymph than blood.

Your blood is pumped from the heart through arteries to thin, porous capillaries where it is defused into this fluid called Lymph.

Your cells have a thinking intelligence. They take the oxygen and nutrients necessary for their health right out of the Lymph and then excrete toxins, some of which return to the capillaries.

The dead cells, blood proteins, and other toxins must be removed by the Lymph system. The Lymph system is activated by deep breathing. The blood has a pump, the Lymph does not. Deep breathing and muscle movement is the travel mode for Lymph, without it, Lymph stagnates. You must stimulate the Lymph to maintain health.

Dr. Jack Shields put a camera inside people's bodies to see what stimulates the cleansing of the Lymph system. He discovered deep, diaphragmatic breathing is the most effective way to accomplish this. It creates a vacuum that sucks the Lymph nodes through the blood stream and multiplies the pace in which the body eliminates toxins. Deep breathing increases this process up to fifteen times.

Studies done by Nobel Prize winner, Dr. Auto Warberg, director of the Maxplank Institute for Self Physiology, showed how healthy cells deprived of oxygen turned malignant.

Dr. Harry Goldblat, in 1953's issue of the *Journal of Experiential Medicine*, showed where he used a species of rats never known to have malignant cells. He divided them into three groups. He put one group in a bell jar and deprived them of air for thirty minutes. Many cells died, some slowed movement, others took on the structure of malignant cells.

After 30 days he injected the malignant cells into the three groups of rats. After two weeks the rats that were not deprived of air were fine. The rats that were deprived of air developed malignant growths. A year later the normal cells were still normal, the malignant cells remained malignant.

One in three Americans contract cancer, but only one of seven athletes do. Whether you are 100 or 400 pounds, you are six trillion cells. It is not how many cells that's important, it's what they carry.

Set one or two times aside daily for deep breathing exercises. This is compatible with the driving of an auto, but certainly not to breathe so deep and hold it so long that you hyperventilate.

EXERCISE:

Breathe in through the nose to four or five counts of your heartbeat, hold the breath in to twelve counts, breathe out through the mouth to the count of eight to ten, hold the breath out to the count of twelve. Repeat this process nine more sets.

Within three days of this exercise, give attention to the changes in your body or temple that will take place. Your breathing will already become more balanced and regular. Your level of energy will have increased, depending on certain circumstances, and your sex drive will increase, also according to circumstance.

After a few weeks, you may even notice your shoulders have raised. Do your shoulders slump because you lack energy or do you lack energy because you allow the shoulders to slump? Please feel free to cogitate upon this question. Before I go into meditation, I begin by breathing in deeply and smoothly through the nose and slowly release the breath through the mouth while focusing all my attention on the breath at the nostrils, not following it in or out, but keeping the focal point of attention on the breath at the nostrils. Three sets total, more if needed.

Keep in mind that you are breathing in life for life. I question any method of meditation that would intentionally exclude deep breathing exercises.

Another breathing exercise that increases your level of energy and feeling of connectedness:

Focus on the heart, visualize going into your temple there, sitting on a golden throne with a feather pillow on it. As you sit and sink into the comfort, deeper and deeper, you notice feathers have blown into the air surrounding you so that you begin to breathe very slowly and smoothly between the feathers, so they don't get in your nose; breathe in through the nose, out through the nose. Continue this controlled breathing for one minute and repeat it, as needed, to still the mind. It is immediately effective in stilling the mind, as you will discover. Two or three breaths; very deep, but gentle, in this mind set will truly still the body and mind.

Before we give additional meditation exercises, I will show you, in living mind, how visualization works—with your participation of course.

Without looking around, count the doors in your house, close your eyes. Now! Okay, go back into the mind and imagine the most stimulating of sexual experiences you've had. This time for two to three minutes. We think in symbol form, intended thought is controlled visualization.

Oh, by the way, if you find sex a poor example for visualization because you think it's dirty or evil, I would suggest you bathe before having it—and remember how you arrived here.

Now, with the power of your new-found imagination, allow me to share a true story with you.

There was a man who learned the secret of imagining. After small successes, he went to a larger goal, five thousand dollars, to be specific. In the 30's that was enough to buy a house and a few cars. He began daily to focus on a five thousand dollar check. He would create and recreate the image of this check. He would picture himself receiving the check, spending the money, buying the house, etc. He did this daily for months until one day his boss at the factory where he labored for a meager living, called him into the office and presented him with a five thousand dollar check and some release forms to sign.

The man had been off work for awhile and some of the time off was spent in a hospital. You see, the five thousand dollar check was compensation for the hand he lost in one of the machines out in the plant.

Makes you want to sit down, right now, and meditate on money, doesn't it? The moral here is faith without deeds could become a real mess. So play the Lotto, join Shaklee, go to bingo games, give more of yourself in service to others, but do something that has the potential to play as the vehicle through which you may obtain your vision or goal, be it money, home, relationship or whatever you desire.

Now, more than ever on this planet, goals are manifesting by the truckload and at an unbelievable rate of speed.

EXERCISE (Kingdom, power and glory)

Focus your attention on the center of your heart. Visualize your entire chest area enveloped in a pink cloud.

Hold this visualization as you breathe in to the count of six.

Hold your breath to the count of ten or twelve, as you raise the pink cloud just above your head.

Release your breath to the count of eight as you expand the pink cloud around your entire upper body.

Hold your breath out to the count of twelve as you continue to visualize the bright pink cloud. Focus on your throat area, visualize a bright blue cloud around your throat and shoulders.

Breathe in to six.

Hold to twelve, as you raise the blue cloud just above your head.

Release your breath to eight as you expand the blue cloud around the upper body.

Hold your breath out to twelve as you visualize the bright blue cloud enveloping your entire upper body.

Now focus on the top center of your head, breathe in to six as you visualize a most brilliant white light around your head.

Hold to twelve as you gently raise the light just above your head.

Release to eight as you expand the light.

Hold your breath out to twelve as you imagine the entire room light up as if the sun just rose in the middle of it.

Sit in complete quietude for no less than five minutes.

Then after the silence, petition something you desire. Example: "Almighty 'I AM' Presence, I call forth _____." *(fill in this part with your intent, goal, or desire)*.

Then say, "Let good befall the world." Then rise, letting go of all you've done from mind, so it may make its rounds.

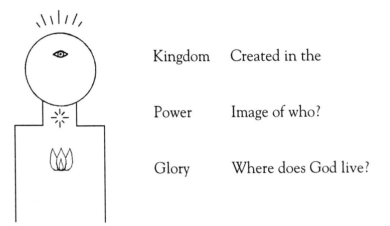

Kingdom   Created in the

Power   Image of who?

Glory   Where does God live?

MANTRAS

I have discovered that mantras only work if you use them. They not only raise your vibrations, but all upon Mother Earth as well, to include her. Keep in mind that the power is not in the mantra. The power is in the director.

FOCUS: In the center of the brain, intone the sound of "err" or "urr."

EFFECT: Clears confusing thoughts, helps to bring focus of singular thought or no thought.

FOCUS: On the heart center. Intone the sounds of Ra Meh, Ra Ma, Ra Meh seven times, repeat three times.

EFFECT: Helps you feel your true oneness with whole, I, Spirit.

FOCUS: On the heart center, the very center, and picture your alter, the threefold flame: blue, gold, red, 1/16 inch tall, so far in most of us. In your mind you may recite, "I open, balance, blaze, expand the threefold flame within my heart." Then intone the sound of "ALA Ohm" or "Amaroosh" seven times, repeat three groups of seven.

EFFECT: The feeling of oneness.

FOCUS: On the brow of your head at the pituitary gland, 1 1/2″ deep within the skull. Intone the sound of "AUM." Make the "M" sound three times longer than the "Au" or "Ah."

EFFECT: Psychic enlightenment, "The light of the body is the eye." This eye, the Ajna.

I recommend Ra Ma every chance you get, one of Gandhi's favorites. It means "to rejoice," same meaning for the word Jesus. Recite silently.

FOCUS: On the right side of your head just above and behind your right ear (area 39). Intone the sound "Ma-Na" or "Man-new" for two or three minutes.

EFFECT: Memory, "Remember Who You Are."

FOCUS: On the pituitary and pineal body's, center of brain. Intone "Ohm" (OM). Make the M sound three times longer than the O sound.

EFFECT: Awakening to your spiritual power. Activates pituitary gland, pineal body, and heart center.

FOCUS: On the area a couple of inches above the top center of your head, known as "The Sacred Lotus Blossom," the crown chakra, or the kingdom of the most high mind in you. Intone the sound "Hue" (Hu). For a profound uplifting, intone this for up to 20 minutes.

EFFECT: Soul travel and connecting with the "I AM Christ Consciousness." I recommend you do not get hung up on these exercises. As a matter of perception, I admonish you not to make them a ritual of biding your time or just performing them as a fill-in or "Well, let's experiment a little."

The key here is, mean it when you do it or don't do it. The mantra is not the power, you are. It is the tool, as need be, to awaken you to SPIRIT.

Your best results will show in your daily life as you observe the gradual change or transformation. One very important ingredient is to always pour in ample amounts of love when performing any spiritual exercises. Love of God/Universe, self, others, enemies included, Mother Earth, mother-in-law and anything whatsoever that comes to mind when performing these exercises.

It is most helpful to refocus on the area of concern each time you begin the intonement of the mantra. To keep unwanted thoughts from clouding your focus while performing these mantras, mentally repeat sayings like, "open, balance, blaze and expand my pituitary gland" or "I join, bond, connect, expand my pineal body and pituitary gland."

The way in which you expand your level of awareness that will work best for you is not necessarily the way I practice, teach, or preach it, but is in truth not mine, but your truth. It is good for only but one individual, the one who actively experiences the performing of the principles of ask, seek, and knock. To no one will the door remain closed.

For the " I AM Presence, GOD" to come through, you must do as His boy instructed, "Peace, Be Still," clear your mind. I don't recommend to force the mind, but the body, yes, if that's what it takes to make meditating a part of your day, especially as you awaken to it and just before you retire from it.

You will soon enough realize what's been missing in your relationships. It's not a soul mate you seek, that's your "out here" thoughts. It's because you are not going within to mate with your soul that is the missing link. As you go in and touch your soul, all of it, you will all of a sudden become aware of more soul mates "out here" than what you could now imagine possible. When I say relationships, I refer to it all, all of life. You are related to it all, this is how you make that discovery. Love towards it all.

Don't be a thinkin' that once you have meditated haphazardly for a few months that you need not sit any more. Don't be naive. There are races in the universes advanced hundreds of thousands of years beyond us that sit the first four hours, for meditations, each day. They don't wait till Sunday to pay the piper, they pipe it in daily. They live consciously in the higher dimensions and so too can you. Your meditations should be in segments of no less than fifteen minutes, eventually thirty or more will become desired by the devoted meditator. Keep your meditations simple, but make them a habit, which they say takes twenty-one days to form. The single most important thing to remember about meditating is to do it daily until you live it.

Let me share a few short, true stories that happened to me after I became a fixed-in-meditation kinda' guy.

When I was at Sedona's red rocks for a couple of months becoming meditative; one morning during a prayer part of meditation, I asked to see God that day. I left it at that, without imagining how, just knowing it possible.

I climbed down off the mountain, headed to my favorite restaurant on the downtown strip of Sedona. I parked, walked in and the waiter seated me. I must admit I hadn't even thought of what I asked for previously that morning in meditation. Well, as the waiter seated me, I couldn't help but notice the two year old li'l girl staring at me as she was turned around in her chair, holding on to the back of the chair with both hands and a smile so far across her face it could melt steel.

The waiter brought water. I noticed out of the corner of my eye, the li'l girl was still looking my way. The waiter took my order, it was easy, O.J. and breakfast bar. I noticed the little girl had not moved her position. I turned enough to see her mother and father on both sides of her, since she was on the end of the table. They had both called her name to finish her meal. She didn't budge.

At that point, it dawned on me that what I asked to see in my meditation that morning was, in fact, before me. I calmly turned to the li'l girl, looked into her eyes and said, "Hello Big Daddy."

She screamed with laughter and immediately turned her attention to her parents and went back to eating her meal.

Now, Big Daddy was not the name her parents called her, but it felt more appropriate to me than saying, "Hello God," with both parents there. This was one of those incredulous scenes that, for your own confirmation, you would have to be in the experience.

The next confirmation was on top of the same peak, viewing distance just southeast of Enchantment Resort where I so often went to do my morning and evening meditations.

There I was, after tuning up the birds, bees, and trees with my flute, deep in meditation for over an hour when my attention was being drawn away from within to without by the constant stare of a male human about my age at the bottom of the peak.

I opened my eyes and shifted left to see him squinting and staring right at me. I went back into meditation. At least five minutes elapsed. My attention interrupted again, I opened my eyes to see him still staring at me.

I wanted, at that point, for he and his family to know I didn't claim ownership of the rock where I sat. I yelled down to him, "There's room for about twenty people up here." He began to climb up. After arriving at the top where I sat, he was attempting to say good morning between deep breaths, trying to catch his wind. He breathed in a big breath and said, "MAN YOU'RE TURNING THE WHOLE MOUNTAIN BLUE!"

He began explaining how his auric sight came to him after some time of performing an exercise system someone had previously shown him. After a while, he offered to show me so we climbed down and he showed me five exercises that, ever since, I have performed every single day beginning about July 1, 1995. Soon after, I learned what he was performing is called the "five rites." You may learn it properly in a book titled, *The Ancient Secret to the Fountain of Youth,* or more properly, in a book titled *Jewel in the Lotus.*

Another confirmation of the power and reality in meditating was on the same peak that, by the way, is high enough that the bugs don't bother you there at all.

One night about ten o'clock, I was in a deep meditative state. It was a beautiful cool night. Something exterior pulled my attention from the state of bliss I was experiencing. It was normal for me by this stage of my meditation progress to get a buzz or glowing sensation, but it never before sounded quite like the one drawing my attention up above my crown chakra, which I had been very focused on that particular night.

To my surprise, as I opened my eyes, there were hundreds of bugs. As I viewed them, I could see many were definitely of the mosquito family and there is a special attraction to my blood type by these li'l critters, but not one bit me that night.

I began to consider the alternative motive. These bugs being trained at the carnival to be vegetarians was not one of the possibilities in my consideration. So what do bugs attract to at night? "LIGHT!" Where was my focus? At the crown chakra, just above the head, visualizing light coming down into my head.

The insects were swarming in a circular and clockwise motion, no closer than a foot from the top of my head like a small tornado shape. As I looked up to them, they began to disperse. As I returned to the meditation, they returned. One more confirmation of the truth in meditation. Light is there even when you don't see it.

I have tried many methods of meditation off and on, mostly off, since I was thirty. One day, long about August 1994, I planted my gluteus maximus on a chair for one hour a day minimum and continued for five months consecutively until force was no longer necessary. I no longer imagined living on this beautiful planet without going within what She loaned me as a vehicle of expression every single God-made day—being glad in it has become me.

At this same period, I was including St. Germaine in my studies and meditations. Each morning and evening for a couple of weeks, I asked La' con te' de' St. Germaine to surround me in the violet flame hundreds of times. Shortly before this, I learned that Leonardo da Vinci said, "Violet increases the power of meditation by ten times." Well, here is my personal experience with purple.

During the day, as I was taking aura photos of people at one of the metaphysical bookstores, this li'l girl, I'd say age eleven to twelve walks up. I had a lady in the chair, ready to snap her photo. The li'l girl looked at the lady in the chair and said, "She's blue with a little..." I don't recall the other colors she exclaimed. Then she looked above my head toward the ceiling and said, "God, you're purple!"

When one uses that title to address me, the recall is more permanent. I must say that I was not surprised. She was one of eight people who claimed that I was emitting purple within that week.

About a week passed, I was in the same store. A guy walked up to me, looked at me, then around and above me. I was drawn to his eyes the whole time. They were brown, beautiful, warm, and sincere. I had no doubt of what was on the other side of those eyes. I said, "I'm David, as I extended my hand. Glad to meet you."

He said, "I know."

Just then his friend stepped up beside him and said, "I'd like to introduce you to the world's greatest channeler. "I was still fixed on his eyes. I said, "How did ya' know." He looked down, just below my chin and said, "your name tag."

We got a big laugh out of that one. Instant friendship.

He said, "You're white and gold."

That caught me off guard. In my mind, I questioned the wisdom behind "those eyes." Gold, huh?"

He repeated, "Yeah, white above you and gold over here and here," lookin' at my left side and throat area.

As you have discovered by now white and gold are preferred colors, so I was pleased in a way, and in another way puzzled—wondering what happened to my purple. I didn't say anything to him about it. I asked him if he would mind if I checked his auric viewing ability.

Most people that see the aura don't register it that well. They usually only see hazy, fuzzy light and not all, if any, color of it. Up to this point, I had met about fifty or sixty people who see auras. Since then, I've met a total of two hundred plus. The fella' said, "Sure."

I stepped over to the closest human and whispered in her ear what I was going to do, so she could also witness his claims.

The fella', I do not recall his name, said, "Stand by that white wall."

He explained that light backgrounds give you a better viewing of the aura, so I did. I immediately went into a closed eye, silent meditation and mentally began to repeat, "Beloved St. Germaine, surround me with the violet flame," over and over. I must have repeated it twenty times; the whole time, thinking of a bed of violet flowers like I often do in meditations. After a minute, I asked, "How does my white and gold look now?"

He was squinting a little, looking at my left side as he said, "Your gold is almost gone behind all the purple coming over it."

Along with the gold, my doubt of his ability vanished. I certainly had my reasons to question the abilities of the claimed channelers in Sedona, Arizona. I had met several who were functioning on about ten percent self, and ninety percent outside forces. I suppose channeling is okay if you are grounded, but personally, I prefer to inhabit my own vessel. I make one exception. I will explain in a minute. Anyway, this fella' of wisdom, showed me how to view the auras around the people in the store. Only one other time in my life had I seen auras so clearly. That was around a great teacher I had known named Mary.

I believe being in his aura enhanced my ability while he was near. He had me look across the room at a lady and said, "Now squint, now relax.

As I did, I very clearly saw her green as I said, "Green."

He said, "Yep, right side."

I confirmed.

I was giving a seminar at what you might call a very open-minded church once and a fella' was telling me the names of the different beings he channels. He finally stopped and looked at me funny. He noticed that I wasn't really getting into his conversation. He asked,

"Do you channel?"

I said, to his relief, "Sure do."

He asked, "Who do you channel?"

I replied, "Only one, and as a matter of fact before I ever get up for public speaking, I ask him to do it all for me so the people receive the best message possible."

He said, "Who's that?"

I replied, "I go direct—God—but His son may enter any time."

Then he seemed to run out of questions and conversation.

At this point, I will say that for those of you who believe the idea that affirmations, decrees, prayers, or spoken words don't matter much, you're right! Yours won't if that is your conviction. I have attempted to express the significance of these creative gifts of power and I can certainly understand that there may be a lot less effort on your part to believe along these lines; but with that lessor effort, shall be less results. No seeds, no crops.

There is so much more to say on the power and soul's profit in meditating; so many ways, forms, methods, etc., but you can know them all if you but apply the single most important ingredient of meditation, ...DO IT! Go unto your Source.

Meditation is not an option for peace of mind. If you are not going within, you are going without! When is the best time for you to step out of your way and into your Presence? Stop looking to appearance! Start looking to the PRESENCE! Not for just some, or most, but for all things in your life. The reason NOW is the best time is because there ain't no other time. The only time you shall ever experience, here on earth or heaven, will be as it has always been, NOW!

The answer to all of it is here. You've carried it with you every step of the way. However, to know, you must think it out, act it out, speak it out, and live it out. HERE, NOW! For those good metaphysicians who think they need not still the body and mind from the outer in a sit-down, turn-off, be-still kind of atmosphere, but seem to believe that you may just be meditative all day and that will do it; let me ask, if this be all you are doing to touch Source, is it working well for you yet?

He/she who hath a constructive, motivated momentum, initiating it with the force of the will, existence shall add to you, but you must initiate. It is only you who can initiate the call. How many lives have you been waiting for it just to happen by chance so far? You cannot ascend from the flesh lest you be in it. You would not be in it if you didn't desire it, and you shall not evolve out of it until you reverse the charge.

I was 43 years of age when I began to sit down and meditate each and every day. I was already with some white/gray hair at 40. At 41, I had a patch of white on either side of the front area of my head. After meditating for 5 months, I had only a few strands of gray hair left. I'm 45 as I edit this book for its second printing. I've never colored my hair and now have no white or gray.

If you are in the understanding of the three most basic laws of the universe you will "get it."

#1   THE LAW OF MAGNETIC ATTRACTION

The most powerful of all laws (just the way it is). You magnetize to you what you allow your thoughts to dwell upon. What is your attention on? This is what you are drawing.

#2   THE LAW OF DELIBERATE CREATION

If you are not intending what you do want, you will receive "whatever" through default. Another way of receiving something you don't want is to really, really, really *not* want it, then you shall really get it.

#3   THE LAW OF ALLOWANCE

If you are not allowing, you are resisting. There is no fine line here. Resisting is most disempowering and burns excessive amounts of energy. There is no evolutionary growth of co-creating in resistance of any kind.

If you recall the recommendation stated in the bible, "Above all things I wisheth that you go out and resist everything" was not what was said. Nor did it say, "Above all things I wisheth that ye go through life cursing your material manifestations, feeling sickly, settling for less than you desire, or denying the five senses I blessed you with."

EXERCISE

Light a candle, sit comfortably. Search your thoughts for good memories—that new bike as a child, graduation, new car, a day in the park. Select good memories only and dwell on them for 68 seconds consecutively. This may take quite awhile and several practices. No matter how well your performances as you hold these good 'feelings" in your vibration, you raise it to a degree.

After holding it for awhile, verbalize any wishes, desires, or decrees you are wanting to the universe. Then be still for five minutes, stand and let it go. Your mind will make you think this is a long five minutes—don't give it a thought. It is your mind you are training or retraining.

I want to say to you here; I mean not to imply that you should attempt to apply every method I teach in these writings. Use what you feel you need, at the time of that feeling or need.

I've given you a pretty good lecture on being disciplined about these practices. Yes, do, but enjoy the experience, have fun with it, and don't become compulsive about it.

Being in a state of appreciation is a vibrational equivalency to feeling good.

* * * * *

Now what would God say about all this?

Remember Who You Are

ᴄWhat ᴄWould God Say?

"A wise man will hear, and will increase learning: and a man
of understanding will attain unto wise counsel."

Proverbs 1:5

ime has arrived on our planet to awaken to our own personal divinity. It is now illegal to burn humans for being special or different and stoning them to death, at least by rock throwing, is a bit out of fashion. It's time to return home and I am not talkin' leave the farm, ranch, house or apartment.

I refer to the raising of self to the higher vibrational state of mind some call heaven. I don't mean, maybe later if you qualify. I refer not to a place where the saints go marching home. I mean right here in your mind, right now, right smack dab in the center of eternity. I call this idea—that heaven is a place later, the "maybe later syndrome" or "post dramatic illusion."

You must bring your lower self to the surrender of this higher vibratory level of mind power so it can and will press out through the cellular structure of your body now while you are in it.

Jesus was not Christ, or not conscious of it, until He brought Himself unto it through baptism; the erasing power of the mind, not just a dunk in the river. He showed us that we must dump, "cast down," the ways of mankind's fears, possessions, and as His promise, if you do it the way He did, follow me, you too shall become the Christ, God, activated through material form.

"I go unto my Father." (Meditate). Where think you He went to visit God? He taught us God is an indoor kinda activity. Life itself comes from inside the tiny seed of the mighty oak tree. So too, lives your power of faith inside your house. Your mind has been conditioned to use it or not. Shakespeare made this point: If you deny Christ consciousness, "Father-Source," it will deny you equally.

Take advantage of this new era, identify with your Almighty "I AM" Presence, "God Source." It is everything you are and vice versa. In the animating, bringing to life, of your spiritual gifts, you must reprogram any programs based on fear and its related negative qualities. To do this, you must denunciate who you are not, "I AM NOT fear, guilt, shame, unworthy, anger, etc." Then you must remember who you are and affirm it in the first person. "I AM ONE WITH THE ALL."

Let's do a little arithmetic. God plus Jesus equals two, right? God plus Jesus plus Holy Spirit equals three, right? God plus Jesus plus Holy Spirit plus you equals four, right? WRONG! Would you like me to call these "problems," as do your teachers here? Let me assist you in solving this simple adding problem. These all added together along with everything you have ever heard, saw, smelled, touched, felt, or sensed in any way, and everything else that is, adds up to ONE! Call it as you will, God is all that is. He may be expressing life through you and your dog and the fallen angel, but there exists only

ONE.

Ya' know I never had any idea that a book so well written could come through a guy like me. I suppose it never would have unless I had stepped out of my way and into my presence. At the age of forty, I began to invoke the God presence within. Little by little, lesson by lesson, turmoil, depression, and heartbreak began to gradually re-form and reshape my life; especially when I began to view these things as experiences that could not harm me whatsoever. They could only make me feel. Deny it or not, they make you feel. Until you realize it is the "God Presence" way of shifting you to higher acts of expression, it will continue as negative in your perception. Once you begin to talk back to these feelings, and talk back I did, asking why, what, where, and how, the universe will begin making life clear for you.

I sat down and had a talk with my feelings about dominion and told them I am taking mine back! It wasn't so much my life that was changing, as my perception of it. I kept provoking the God Force. I never missed at least one hour in meditation each day. This went on month after month. I was sick and tired of being sick and tired. I wanted answers! I demanded answers! I yelled at God! I screamed at God! I even told Him to get a life. You know what He said?

"BE GLAD TO MY SON, GIVE ME A BODY."

I finally said, "Come on down." I mean, what else could I say to that?

It began to dawn on me that God is not some big bad dude in the sky awaiting my demise so that He can get His wrathful hands on me and punish me for all my sins. I began to realize that what I termed "God" is the universal source available to us to the degree or level of our acceptance of it.

Do you realize what happens to your life when you begin making statements like, "From the Almighty 'I AM' presence I call forth clarity. I step aside, you lead the way." Of course not, how could you unless you have experienced the doing of it. Same ol' seeds, same ol' crop; new seeds (thoughts), new crop (life). If you give way to new ideas, whether in my book, what you hear, or in your heart and you invoke them with meaning and faith that they already belong to the real you, your life will not only get better, but never again slide back quite as far, ever!

Each and every time you come unto memory of who you are, big or little, you have obtained to a higher level of vibration and expansion of mind. Out of the coma the amnesia fades, your awareness quickens and you will eventually, once and for all time, remember who you are. No matter how far off the path of light, no matter how low you have stooped to dishonor your true self in illusions, YOU ARE OF THE MOST HIGH!

Another aspect of myself I had no idea about was this: Along about the age of 42, I picked up a flute at one of the crystal stores in Sedona where I was doing aura readings. I bought a cheap bamboo or cane flute that I would take to the rocks where I meditated, and just played around with it. After several months, I got good at it— very good. I began to play some of the better flutes in the stores where I worked. As I would sit awaiting customers while reading a good book, I often noticed shoppers eyeing or picking up the flutes and other musical instruments. I got to where I would walk up to them, put a same note flute in their hands and mine and say, "Watch me. Now do this." Many would catch on quickly.

I noticed that my skills improved as I met some children ages 8-12 who came from up the street at the Boys and Girls Club of Sedona looking for "something to do." One of the store employees was talking about kicking them out for loitering, but being that these li'l ones had become my friends and truly good acting, mannered kids, I would have them each get a flute and take it to the little crystal room in the back where we wouldn't be a bother to others. We would all play in unison as they caught on. After a couple of months, five or six of these kids who were expected to be trouble-makers were beginning to sound like a band. I don't recall all their names, but Jessica was kinda' their leader and a real cool kid.

I now teach many how to play most instruments, because as I began to assist others in their goals and unfolding of their talents, I discovered mine. I discovered 'long about 43-45 that I can make musical sounds with most instruments on this planet—many of which I now play very well.

No matter how "bad" you believe yourself to be with something, as you assist others in it, you will get better, and eventually discover you have gifts/talents you never knew you had. You must act it out. When will you be coming up?

All things that have been accomplished by the great gurus, so shall you do. You and the Father are one, you are in Him as He is in you. You who take up meditations on the most high in your heart and head, shall have and be added to. The almighty kingdom, power and glory reside within the cellular structure of your temple (body). When you meditate, draw near, to your "I AM" presence, as you are in quietude, it shall draw nearer to you. Let that divine mind be in you—contemplate light. Awaken that part of you that sleepeth. Become the creator you incarnated to be; stop blaming and running around scared of God and start creating with Him. Focus, in your meditations, on the crown chakra (top of head), and your whole body shall be filled with light. Deny no part of your beingness and it will deny no part of you. I beseech you to invoke your spiritual gifts, psychic powers. I admonish you not to cast your new pearls before swine (brag to humans still living in fear). They will judge you in their fear and try to hang you as did they to their previous saviors. A closed mind only knows of heaven, but may not enter.

Let the dead bury the dead. Jesus attempted to bring His people to the higher vibrations of life and what did they bring Him to, for it, out of their fear of the unfamiliar? The cross. Now you hear their justifications for their dastardly deed. They say, "Oh the Lord sent His son so we could kill Him and be saved from our sins." If you can for a moment, sink down to that level of "BS." You may have been one of the advocates of the Lynch mob, so forgive yourself, cancel out, and be born of the Spirit. How on earth, in body, can the process of allowing Spirit to manifest through your body with a brick wall of fear, guilt, and shame in the way ever work?

We interrupt this chapter to bring you a special enlightenment.

This is not a development course nor a school lesson; school you go to when you need to know something you don't already know. The design and intent here is to awaken you to the awesome power of who you already are. The part of you that already knows. As soon as you let go of judgment toward self and others, applied by and taught by self or others; what you term a miracle shall light upon you. Judgment must be eliminated. It is not optional. It is equal to anti-Christ, the drawing away from your own Christ self within.

The way in which you remember who you are is to identify with your savior, the Christ within you. In your daily meditations, affirm, "Beloved Father, reveal Christ, your perfect son to me, bless you Christ." Because some think these processes not easy, they assume they are difficult. Not true. They may not be easy, but simple enough for the small child. And by the way, the child applies the simplicities of spiritual law quite readily until some well-meaning, ignorant adult teaches them to "be careful, there's not enough," "money don't grow on trees," "fear strangers," etc., etc. Yes, continue to go within daily until you are guided from there. Keep it simple, not ritual. Be glad in each day that the universe has thought up for you. Going within need be not a chore after you have initiated yourself with the benefits thereof, but it is a choice. When they say come forward now, that is because there is literally no other time you can. Now let's see if we can stimulate some memories.

HOW TO SHUT DOWN YOUR HIGH ENERGY CENTERS

Hang around people who express fear, blame, condemnation or speak of lack, want, and limitation or display negative attitudes, judge self or others with hate or resentment. Then go around saying, "Why is this evil always happenin' to me?" Attend any place where anyone teaches that you are an unworthy sinner, rather than a worthy winner, or that you should sit around in the pity party of guilt, shame, or remorse for your imperfections.

If your desire is *not* to shut down your vital energy centers, then be selective in whom you befriend. Know this eartheans, energy is energy, no matter how or where you direct it. If you belong to an organization of any kind that teaches against anything; like for example, another religion, a cult, the devil, hell, or any other thing they call bad, evil or negative, out to get you, consider this: Attention to anything *is belief in that thing.* The degree of attention given is the same amount of worship toward the thing you resist.

How many Gods do you worship? May I be so bold as to ask? Do you wait for a special day of the week? Will it keep you from going to hell by believing in it? Will you get sent there out of spite if you affirm that hellfire and brimstone is a false teaching? Who would do the sending? The devil and his demons, hah! I think not, at least not without permission from Source. Would your own 'father" send you there? Would you send your son? Would you send yourself? Ahh, gettin' warmer.

Now if you can receive the fact that we have been misprogrammed, you might see the necessity in getting reprogrammed. If you don't know you are in prison, why would you try to escape? If you are not in use of your God-given gifts, then you are on the dark side of the wall, a prison of sorts. Why are you here now in three-dimensional form? Do you believe God will grace your return? Did you sin in heaven and get booted? You hate it out here, don't you? Have you ever asked self why you hate it here? God made earth for man, right? Fear will keep you in a vibration incompatible with joy (heaven on earth).

No organization has monopoly rights on God, Jesus, Christ, Lord, Savior, salvation, the Bible, the universe or spiritual law. There are those who act as though they do—those who truly believe they know the only way to get to heaven, as they thump a book written thousands of years ago and written hundreds of years after the experiences described therein took place. Maybe some proclaimed authority on the subject told 'em how it's done, encouraged them to CONVERT, join their membership and become another cult member. Large or small, a cult is a cult. Go ahead, look up "cult" in your Webster, get the knowledge.

Never force any system of belief on any humans, regardless of age or relationship. To guide your children into their truth has nothing to do with guiding them into yours. Does God force Himself on you? Did Jesus force His beliefs on others? Next time you decide to cram your beliefs down your children's throats, consider how much hate or confusion it will cause the child. If you believe in your "control freak" attitude, have button will push, that everyone around you needs salvation, get the understanding of the word's meaning. "Salvation" means, "liberation from ignorance of illusion." If you truly know you have spiritual salvation, would that not spill over into your physical, family, social, mental, emotional and financial life as well? You're scared, almost to death, that you may just barely "not" make it through those pearly gates, hah? The preachers have you scared silly, don't they?

One of the activities that used to really get my goat, was watching someone go around the neighborhood trying to get everybody "saved," maybe they thought heaven was a lonely place or maybe it was just them stars in the ol' crown; like they were on some network multi-marketing program—and their sponsor?... You got it, Big Daddy himself. They are always so concerned about that sweet by-and-by that they are fairly oblivious to the sweet here-and-now.

You see, I have already, under martial rule, taken my precautionary steps to earn rights into those pearly gates later, BUT I WANT MY HEAVEN ON EARTH NOW! Oh I can understand if you have a problem with that, but I don't have a problem with you havin' a problem. You may have your heaven later... maybe?... hopefully? It is not something you earn. Simply, it is an awareness that you need merely realize is already within you NOW! I sure hope like heaven you ain't spent your "one" and "only" whole lifetime going through hell to get to heaven and blew it on account a' someone else misdirected you. I mean, imagine that. You have someone else to blame, but it's too late, you're going down! Pretty scary to a mind filled with fear, hah? Especially if it was one of those close calls where you coulda' made it to heaven and you shoulda' made it to heaven and you woulda' made it to heaven, BUT no-o-o-o, there you are on THE JUDGMENT DAY, for you, because you never looked it up in the Aramaic language Jesus spoke. It was written "A" judgment day, not "THE."

Sorry, too late to explain, here is Big Daddy himself:

"Well hello my son, how was earth life?"

Here you are, scared half outta your boxer shorts, woulda' wet 'em, but you're in a robe and they don't have restrooms here.

About this time, St. Pete whips out a CD ROM, with your SS (social soul) number on it, hands it to God, He plugs it into His IBM (infinitely big memory).

While you are standing around trying your best to look all innocent, God says, *"Ahh, here we have the bad list. Whoops, happens every time, there it went off the hard drive, erased forever. Hey, did you get a look at all that?"*

You reply, "Oh yes Sir, sure did."

"Good! Then let's go on to the good list.

"My records indicate that you quit drinking, smoking, cussing, except for all those times you coulda' said God bless that car, God bless that furnace, God bless that lawn mower, but no-o-o-o, your specific instructions to me, now lookie here at the screen, why on earth did you keep telling me to damn everything you needed to work for you?

"I mean, when I was issuing brains, where were you, down at Union Station? You think them words you used weren't real? Man them things are powerful. They are more real than that voice box they came out of.

"Don't you recall me saying in that book you was totin' around, 'BY MY WORD THIS ALL EXISTS.' I didn't say just some of it, man I said, 'ALL OF IT!' You got to get the small clues in the puzzle guy, and please don't lean on my golden throne. You're gettin' soul prints all over it. Step back a little, 'WATCH OUT!' I just manifested that robe.

"Now, it shows here on the program that you became so good, you was nearly good for nothin'. Why, in my name, were you going around acting all scared of me for? Why, that's the same as gettin' spooked by lookin' in the mirror." (You're just standing around try-

ing to maintain that innocent look.)

"What on earth ever gave you reason to be scared of ol' 'Big Daddy'? I said fear me, yes. I didn't say, above all things I wisheth that you run around scared shitless."

"Tee! Hee! Hee!"

"What are you giggling at?"

"What you just said, I didn't know you could say that."

"Are you kiddin'? Has it ever dawned on you why I sent my boy Webster to your planet? Well, for your information, I happen to have my Webster right here; now lookin' up the word 'fear.' Here 'tis, FEAR, profound reverence and awe, especially toward God, that's me."

"Yeah, but!"

"Hold on just a minute. I'm not finished here. Let's take a look at the word 'reverence,' I mean you humans do get all your facts from a book, right? Ahh, here 'tis, REVERENCE: man that's a lot of E's, bet you didn't know 'E' vibrates to your number five did ya'? Five means freedom, didn't know that either did ya'? Of course not, never looked it up. Anyway, here's the meaning: profound adoring, awed respect. See what I'm trying to tell ya' here son?"

"Do you remember in that book those Hebrews wrote (whatever a Hebrew is) where I said love me first more than any other?"

Yes? Well because I am within you, do you not see by the radiating of love toward me that it will include you? I feel right along with you, in you, through you, just as I do in the Goddess your feet walk on when you are incarnate.

"How in heaven do you think I enjoy all those planets I'm al-

ways creating? By using a telescope? Because of your perception of what I am, what better way than to give it to you in what you best understand, A COMMAND. Best way in the world I could figure to get you all to start loving yourselves again, but no-o-o-o, you gave your soul over to some pathetic nimcompoopoo-head who convinced you to love some wrathful, revengeful, punishing creature off in the stars, out there somewhere, someday. In the meantime, you go running in fear with your head way up where the sun don't shine calling yourself "unworthy." How can you feel any joy? At least you were lookin' within.

"Don't you know how ridiculous that sounded to me? Every time you called you that, you called me that.

"I told you in that book about me, to go within in a thousand and one different ways. That's where I talk to you—in you. I live there for Christ's sake! Your feelings, I AM! But no, you'd go and give your body, mind, and soul over to some doomsday fool trying to fatten' his own little outer ego in his folly with your bucks. Wake up man, I don't live in a church, NO CHURCH! I live in a temple, handcrafted by me.

"You! You are the temple and you take me everywhere you go. I'm just along for the ride, you are the driver. You may turn down any road you prefer. You can get lost anytime you like, just turn in to me, I'll shine you a light but you gotta' look to me, not the road. Try to remember in your next experience, when you feel negative. You are not in highest choice, you are not allowing pure positive energy to flow. You are not in alignment with your core source. This is how I nudge you. When you feel positive what you are

intending is a go ahead, my message to you.

"Anyway, let's get back to the other business at hand. They say we're holding up the line. You know ol' St. Pete and that pearly gate thing he does. He has quite a waiting list at times. Well, back to that bad list."

"But I thought…"

"Yeah, I know what you thought. Yes, all the bad stuff is erased, but you may have heard the term 'cause and effect.' Well, son, by all you have intended, created, un-created and re-created, you have set in motion all the circumstances formatting your next incarnation."

"MY NEXT WHAT? The Bible said we only live once on earth."

"How will I ever teach you anything if you keep thinking you already know so much?

"Now pay attention boy, you're starting to get under my robe. They wrote the book about me, didn't they? You know it would do you good to stay in tune with some of the more updated literature. You think the Bible was the only book on Earth I inspired? Man, I inspire everything, all of it!

"Let me pull it up on my laptop. Here we go. How about the King James version, that's your favorite isn't it?"

"Yes, as a matter of fact, it is."

"Yeah, we'll talk about what ol' King Jimmy did later in another book. For now here it is, Hebrews 9:27, '…and as it is appointed unto men once to die.' Now, if you would catch the key word here, that's die, not live.

"Now let me ask you son, why do you think I sent my boy out to

planet Earth? Do you recall all the times He referred to the phrase,
'cast down'?

"My boy, Jesus, had to go through as many lives on your planet
as it takes for the particular individual to get the clue, so to speak.
You know 'cast down.' Your altered ego, the fallen' angel part of
you must die. Once this happens, you break the cycle of birth-
death, no more fear of death because your illusion of it is illumed
to you!

"There, in fact, is no such thing as death, never has been,
never will be. There is not but LIFE everlasting, eternal LIFE!
What do you think of that fact my son?

"Please don't answer. It may take you a thousand earth years
and do you know how many souls I'd have to come up with in a
thousand earth years, each one livin' only once per bodily incarnation? Well, at an average life span of 69 years per, give or take a
few days, at the average pop of, by then, around the earth year
2997 of ten billion, which is all the souls I allotted for your planet
in the first place.

"Let's see, 1,000 years divided into a 69 year span average, is
14.49 times ten billion. Ahh, here 'tis, one hundred and forty-
four billion, nine hundred million, and maybe a couple of
makeovers. Oh, but keep on adding, that's just one thousand earth
years. You wouldn't want to know how long eartheans have been
inhabiting the earth now would you?

"Well, let's say givin' it the benefit of your limited way of thinking, your science is now negotiating, if I may use such a gentle
term for it, whether man has been there one or six million years,

six being the more recent discovery. Well, even at one mil, take that times your previous figures. We're talkin' more souls than you have cells!

"Oh, I heard that thought loud and clear."

"But you're God, I thought you could do anything?"

"Well, let me ask you, do you believe I can create that many trillions upon trillions upon trillions of souls through which to express life?"

"Yes sir, sure do, absolutely."

"GOOD, then out of the things you could become on earth like, for instance; a musician, actor, businessman, housewife, doctor, preacher, attorney, judge, forest ranger, cowboy, Indian, leader, teacher, public speaker, writer, news editor, president, boxer, proball player, scientist, king, queen, knight, etc., thousands upon thousands of unique opportunities, do you believe I can create more than one opportunity for you, as the individualized soul being, to express life on that awesome planet of opportunities?"

"Uh-Huh."

"Your solar star, 'SUN,' gave birth to Goddess Mother Earth over four and a half billion earth years ago. Does that seem like enough linear time to experience all the trips to earth you so desire? I sure hope so because she's going into fifth dimension real soon. If Eartheans consciousness continues as it is now, she will have little cosmic choice but to ascend into what you term superconsciousness between 1998 and 2012 of your standard Gregorian calendars.

"Now about the subject of how long humans have occupied

Terra—not one or six million years, but on the earth date of 2013, the figure is 225 million years. Now, as you know the human species to be, that figure is eight and a half million years. Before that it was many breeds of your ancestors from different areas, mostly the Milky Way as you term it to be. Now I suppose you find these figures either staggering or too incredulous to believe.

"I desire for you to get a slight idea on the meaning of my favorite word, 'INFINITE.' So listen here. Your scientists say the Milky Way Galaxy has 100,000,000,000 (one hundred billion) planets within it and the universe has over one hundred billion galaxies with one to four hundred billion planets in each of them. Let me show you, in my favorite number, all but the first two anyhow, what this figure looks like on paper. Here 'tis rounded off to, say, two hundred and fifty billion planets per galaxy average:

25,000,000,000,000,000,000,000 planets.

"Let me ask you here, are you gettin' the picture of 'vast'?"

"WOW!"

"Good, let me give you a sneak preview of infinite. That was how many stars and planets in the universe your science claims is all of it because it's as far as they can put it to their illusion of facts. So far I have created ten to the forty-ninth power of universes, some having more planets than the one you been hangin' 'round. Here's how that looks with my favorite number behind the one:

100,000,000,000,000,000,000,000,000,000,000,000,000,000,000,000,000
UNIVERSES

"Would you like to see the figure that represents the amount of

planets in all my universes?"

"Yeah, sure, you bet!"

"Know the word 'fathom'?"

"Yes."

"You couldn't! I'd love to show you. I just love showing off. My boy's just like me. You know, that water walk thing he did. It runs in the DNA, you know how it is, you've got it. Imagine slowing down enough to enjoy just one of the many planets I have created for your enjoyment, say planet earth for example.

"Now we better get on with this before we miss supper and we'll both be in trouble if we miss the Lord's Supper 'cause I'm the guest of honor and Mother Mary is cookin'.

"Anyway, we can give you amnesty for the bad list and a few stars for the good list, but you shoulda' kept busy on yourself instead of going around trying to save everyone else. It's not your pressure, but example, that lifts spirits. I thought you knew that, you used to say it a lot. The most you did, by preachin' that hell fire stuff, was get a lot of my children scared half out their britches.

"Now finally, my favorite part here, 'THE SENTENCING.' All right, do you have any final words?"

"Yes sir. I believed in your son, Christ, and the Holy Spirit and you and heaven and all that stuff."

"Ya', sure you did, you still do, but you always believed in everything for later instead of in the now and you always thought Christ was some dude somewhere else. I came to see you as 'sonny boy' and told you quite clearly, you have to chose to become the Christ.

"The most prevalent belief you have just now, as I pick this up on my telepathic wave length, is that I'm a big, mean, angry God. So be it! You ever hear the ol' saying, 'as one believes, he conceives or you'll see it when you believe it'?

"I'm beginning to get a li'l out of sorts here thinking about that time your bunch threw that Lynchin' party for my son and didn't ya' hear what he said? 'I and my Father are one.' 'If you have seen me, you have seen my Father.' I prefer to be called Big Daddy, but either way, that was me you all hung with them long railroad spikes. God knows where you got them in that age. I mean, you didn't even have trains yet. Something else the lot of you didn't have much of that rhymes with trains. My instructions were that you love me, not hang me. I guess that's what happens when you go around scared of your own shadow. You all down there, always throwing some kinda' Lynchin' party. Who do you think you are, GOD?

"Now, I realize that you go by John 3:16 and have your heart set on that promise; but let me ask ya', do you believe in that eternal damnation, burning in hell thing?"

"Yes Sir! Whoops, what's happening? I'm sinking. Oh my, I'm going down into a tunnel ...HELP! Oh, wow! It's gettin' hotter. I just knew this was gonna' happen. OOPS! Ouch! Oh! I've landed somewhere. Man it's hot as Hell down here! Someone get my attorney on the phone. Uh oh! There's that big red-horned flaming guy. I just knew he'd be here. Oh! Gross, look at all these people in chains. This really sucks. Ouch! Hey let go of me! Hey! Your hands are burning the suit buddy. Have you ever looked in a mirror or would it reflect something so ugly? You oughta' to be in an ugly contest, I mean, God, you're ugly!"

"I'm what?"

"OOPS!"

"Did someone call my name?"

"Oh my God! I'm going through another tunnel, not this again, at least I'm going up, Ahh! Ahh, it's gettin' cooler! Oh wow! I'm back!"

"Ahh, someone did call my name. So you're back. How was your visit down there?"

"Are you kiddin? I don't ever want to do that again."

"That's your choice my son."

"What do you mean, my choice?"

"I can see you're gonna' need to join one of our TM (Transcendental Meditation) *classes to get your thinker under control and let me ask the questions for now. Do you believe in more than one God?"*

"I plead the fifth! I mean, if you have that here."

"I must admonish you, my son. Do you recall the written messages that advised you—what is on your mind will become your experience?"

"Ahh, I think so, but what are you getting at?"

"Do you recall the writings that indicated the fact that 'as you thinketh, you shall become'?

"Oh, yeah, sure."

"Do you believe it?"

"Well, Ahh."

"Well, Ahh, while you contemplate it, I'll give you some re-
minders. I sent you many teachers on the subject; like my boy
Albert Einstein. Here's his interpretation of same; 'Your imagination is a preview of life's coming attractions;' and Parkhurst P.
Quimby; 'What you believe, will happen, whether you are thinking about it or not;' and Ralph Waldo Emerson; 'You become what
you think about all day long;' and Buddha; 'All that we are is the
result of what we have thought. The mind is everything, what we
think we become.'

"Are you gettin' the picture here now?"

"Yes Sir!"

"Good, now do you remember how they wrote that you are created in my image?"

"Yeah."

"Well, your mind is offspring, so to speak, of mine; so therefore,
like me, you have the power to manifest. These laws of the universe apply on earth as well as here. The difference is that when
you think it, act it, or speak it here, you experience it NOW, not
later. Here things manifest as you think them. Has to do with that
'now moment' thing that you humans seldom reflect in.

"It's a good thing you thought of your ol' Big Daddy when you
dropped out on me back there by giving thought to other Gods."

"Excuse me! Other Gods? I wouldn't think of it!"

"Sure would, you just did."

"What on earth do you mean?"

"First of all, I don't mean anything on earth. You're not there
now."

"Oh yeah, I AM sorry."

"Son, did you feel that vibration?"

"Yeah, but I lived in California for a long time. I'm used to the ground shaking, but what was that?"

"It never ceases to amaze me how you humans from the 'West,' select the most powerful, creative, vibrational frequencies in the entire universe and follow it with one of the most detrimental defamations there is."

"You lost me. What do you mean?"

"Did you not hear what you just called yourself?"

"No. What?"

"I AM SORRY."

"What for? You didn't do nuttin."

"Not me Abbot, that's what you just called yourself."

"But my names' not Abbot."

"No and it's not Costello and it sure as heaven ain't Einstein either. Now pay attention to what you say, will ya'? Now let me explain it so even you can grasp it.

"When I ask you if you believe in that hell fire thing, you not only affirmed it, but imagined what the experience is like in such detail that you created life-like circumstances of it."

"Is that what happened back there?"

"Yep, absolutely! Anything you give attention to is worship toward that thing."

"Wow, I never thought of it that way. "

"Everything that comes before you is created by your mind, and once you really get this, you will finally be diligent about 'what IS

ON YOUR MIND.'

"What's a matta'? Did you skip some chapters of the book you all wrote about me? You've got to pay attention boy. You gotta' take your mind off Scramble. Sit! Let's do a simple mantra to smooth your thoughts. Okay, together now, breath in; now, errrrrrrrr, breath in; now, errrrrrrrr, once more, and breath errrrrrrrr."

"Wow! That works well. I'm more clear. How come you didn't have that taught to us in your Bible?"

"Wasn't my book, it's yours, and it was taught and taken out. Remember I mentioned something about King Jimmy, you know James? The Hebrews, Greeks, Romans, not to mention what happened when the English 'control freaks' got a hold of it, and along about 533 AD. The Catholics x'd almost everything on the multi-incarnations you experience."

"Why did they do that?"

"To control the masses. The Bible, books, crystals, ministers, prophets, psychics, and the lot of it, are all tools. I nudged you through them all for you to come home. Do you not recall how many times I urged you and guided you and instructed you to go within for the truth? That directive runs throughout your Bible. But you kept your attention on other's opinions and everything else outside of you instead of inside where I always reside in complete bliss and harmony.

"You kept going for those organizations that continued to impress self-denial upon you. Do you not recall my boy saying, 'If you deny me, I will deny you'? Man, that's Universal Law. How in heaven's name do you expect Christ consciousness to come unto

you if you look outside of yourself and say, 'He's Christ, but I'm unworthy'?

"Okay, now that you're back home, did you wanna' visit that other place anymore? You know Lucifer's Lack of Light Lounge?"

"Oh, no sir, absolutely not! ! !"

"I hear ya', the only Light down there will burn ya'! So lose the fear and hop on the ol' buggy here. We have a few eons before supper.

"Let's go to one of those mansions my boys' been preparing for you and see what you'll be calling home for this experience. By the way, sonny, if you ever want my throne, just think like you're ol' Creator, Big Daddy, and it'll be yourn."

"Say what?"

"Oh yeah, the universe gives according to our level of acceptance. As you remember who you really are, the universe flows through you to that degree. It just so happens that l have remembered who I really am to quite a degree!"

"I'll say, but I can't become God!"

"Not speaking in that term, you won't. It's not to become, it's more in the line of 'to be or not.' Kinda' like my boy, Willie, put it; 'you see when you remember who you really are, you will know who 'l ..AM.' "

"Yea, but this must be a big responsibility you've acquired."

"You could say that, but a slight correction in perception is in order. What would be more proper is that I have acquired the ability to respond."

"How did you do that?"

"I first became Self center."

"You mean you used to be on an ego trip?"

"No, are you being fatuous?"

"Why would you say that, I've lost a lot of weight."

"That does it, your first priority here is gonna' be a reunion with my son, Webster. See here, 'fatuous:' silly. You got it?"

"Yeah."

"Self centered, centered within one's Self. Everything that is, is be-caused from within the center of the being you are being."

"Wow, that's heavy."

"LIGHT!"

"Didn't know you smoked."

"No, I mean LIGHT, it's all LIGHT. You manipulate LIGHT."

"I didn't mean to."

"Yes, I can plainly see that. Let's look up the word."

"Oh, I can tell you the meaning of light, I aced science."

"Yes, I bet you can, and I know you did, but I'm referring to the word 'manipulate.' Ahh here, manipulate; to manage or utilize skillfully.

"LIGHT is always there awaiting you to apply it, use it, shape it, mold it, accept it and after you experience any part of it, it returns unto itself. In order to obtain unto its flow, you must apply its propelling force."

"What's that?"

"LOVE."

"Where do l start?"

"With thyself."

"But in the Bible, you said or they said, 'love you first and most.'"

"Yes and where think you, I live? As I've said, I'm an indoor kinda' guy. Love everything. This is the activation of transmutation.

"During our next experience on earth, remember to love it all. Love each experience by embracement, with allowance of it all. Not tolerance, but the true feeling of allowance. Love your beautiful Goddess Mother Earth and all she provides for your enjoyment. You will obtain permanent higher consciousness.

"In just a few weeks of Earth time, you could become so fixed in the universal flow that you can never again become unaware of who you really are. You must love each and every being, place, thing, circumstance, feeling, you experience. Love each time someone goes in front of you, this may slow you down enough so you enjoy your journey there. Send blessings and love to the ones who get on your bumper or as it were, 'under your skin,' this will test your response or reaction to outer influence and manipulation.

"Remember inner manipulation is the key, not outer. This force of universal love will emerge more and more fully through you, bringing you to a higher level of understanding and perception.

"If you recall, understanding preceded the obtaining of 700 wives for my boy, Solomon. This kind of understanding ain't nothin' to sneeze at, if you know what I mean?"

"Okay, hold it right there! I mean, please? You said my next experience on Earth. You mean I gotta' go back there?"

"We've already discussed this and it's WE!, my son. WE! are going and you will continue this, so to speak, 'out there' experi-

ence for another six hundred lives, as you term it, if need be, until you remember who you really are, as it is within the laws of universe. You brought yourself out there, lowered your vibrations from within. Therefore, you must bring yourself back in here, raise your vibrations, of 'out there' from within."

"Whoa! Whoa! Whoa! I mean just a moment. You said another six hundred lives, you mean I've gone to earth that many times?

"SURE HAVE."

"But I hate it out there. Why most of my life, I had enemies who hated me and I hated them. People out there are selfish, rude, and socially unacceptable. I didn't even like most of the places I lived. I was always havin' car trouble. I went through relationships like Tylenol and then when I did settle all we did was fight. My favorite pets died on me or got killed. My job sucked, but it was 'do it or starve.' I was broke or close to it most a' my life and during all that, I was always trying my best to please God. You're tellin' me I gotta' go back to that six hundred more times?"

"As long as you perceive life as happening to you like this, rather than the truth that you are creator of it, all of it, you haven't yet got the hang of it, so to speak. Until you take back your personal dominion over creation's gift to you, you will continue to be tossed about by what you have, in fact, created.

"Now lookie here son, if you don't get that thinker workin' in a childlike way of believing the simplicity in the application of Source, then you're gonna' have a heap a' trouble out there.

"Many believe they should try to please Source, to them 'GOD.' Therefore, this attitude spills over into other areas of their lives.

So they either become people pleasers or institution pleasers which, of course, are directed by people.

"Now, stay up with me here son. Notice I did not say, don't be pleasant. By all means, be pleasant, but while you're being pleasant to everyone else out there, be pleasant to thine own self.

"Source doesn't want or need you to please it, because Source does not want nor need. Source is what everything is made up of, yes—but you do the making and then you have to live with it in your experience.

"Source is there at your ever-beckoning command to be applied by you just as it is for me. Do you recall in your bible the statement, 'command ye me'?"

"Woo! Woo! Woo! Woo! I thought you were God!"

"Not were son, I AM, I AM Source, as much as I apply it. As much to the degree as I accept and allow Source to express its allness through me.

"One must resonate in harmony with the principles and laws of 'The Great Central Sun' if one is to apply the forces therein. To the degree of synchronicity in application of the 'Great Force,' one may command manifestation, precipitation and creation of the Force. Therefore, create to degree of decree."

"But how do we get this kind of understanding out there?"

"Thousands of books and lives out there could not convey to you the understanding of Source as long as you remain in the fear-based limitations of the outer appearance of human thought.

"Source is always asking what next experience will you desire through her."

"Her?"

"Just pay attention, son, we're gettin' to the good part.

"Your greatest teacher is established by thoughts energized with the most feeling involved or dwelt upon the most often. Experience always follows its creator—your thoughts. After the seeded thought was accepted by you, of you being separate from Source, GOD, in your understanding, this seed of separateness was born into your experience. This became, as titled, 'seed for thought.'

"These seed-thoughts beget offspring of like kind. These seeds having in their code the idea of separation, festered and grew into your kingdom of idealism, creating variations of ideas. Some of which caused you to believe such things as you actually have enemies because your Self, 'Higher Self,' imposed freewill. Your lower vibrational bodies were automatically compelled to accept this idea as truth.

"This is why I, as your own higher vibratory consciousness, urged you to love your enemy. This will reunite you with your thought-seeds of separateness, transforming them into the allness through opposite polarity, reunion, heightening your vibratory frequencies back up to the awareness in full consciousness, of the God 'I AM,' you are. If you will love your enemy, will it not then be quite effortless to love everyone else?

"But—priorities first. As I stated in what is termed your 'commandments,' love thyself first and most. That is thy Highest Self, the God 'I AM,' You are within or vice versa.

"Go ahead, give it a test. See if you can love yourself more than Source. I assure you, it shall not come to pass. There is no hurry.

You may repeat this similar life style. We have eternity to do this you know."

"Do what?"

"Bring my kingdom to the outer most consciousness of Hu-man (God-man). You remember the plan don't you?"

"No, but I'm sure you'll remind me."

"Well, actually that's where my son, Jesus, comes in. He has such a way with words. I told you back there to call me Big Daddy and that's just because I've been at this creating business more than you. That is the only reason you view us as different. We're the same.

"You just gotta' get conscious of it by accepting more universal flow. Of course, you will be receiving that now for your stay here. You'll be so recharged with vital force after a few eons or so here. I couldn't keep you from returning to Earth, your home away from home, as long as you desire to roleplay hu-man."

"But a few eons could be the year 5,000, 6,000 or 7,000 AD. I want to experience what's going on there in the 2,000 era."

"What? I can do all this for you and you think I couldn't place you in a specific frame of Earth time? Boy, do you have a lot to remember. Here's an excellent affirmation as remedy for that particular blockage."

> *From the Almighty I Am Presence,*
> *I call forth clarity in my life now.*
>
> *I Step aside and allow my divine plan to unfold,*
> *"God expressed."*

Be still and know that "I AM" God,
  The purest Christ,
  Divine eternal living love and light.

I AM the Christ, son of the most high living God.

I AM the resurrection of the Violet Flame.

I AM the Christ, son of the living God I AM.

I AM Creator, Creation, Spirit in it all.

I AM absolute perfection of my Universal Law.

I AM the wings of the eagle that he may soar.

I AM unlimited universe and many more.

I AM infinite, immeasurable, intelligence, mind divinity.

I AM all that is, all that was and all that ever will be.

I AM the truth that sets my children free.

I AM the life inside the seed that grows to be the tree.

The same out pressing I AM in thee.
  You hear me in your music.
  You taste me in your sweets.
  You see me walking down your streets.
  You smell me in your flowers so sweet.
  You touch me as you feed me treats.

I AM the feelings within your heart that beats.

I AM every breath of air you breathe.
  Don't you see? I've never left you all alone.

I AM everything you've ever known.

When will you be coming home?

I AM health, wealth and prosperity,

> *happiness, joy, success and peace,*
> *beauty, love and harmony.*
> *The Great Central Sun, in thee, I be.*

> *I AM you, as you are me.*

> *I AM whatever you desire to be.*
> *Your bondage I so clearly see.*
> *Use my love to set you free,*
> *and once again "I," you, shall be.*

"Here, I'll tell you what. I'll set your schedule from Earth year 1998 to 2998."

"Wow! Back up, didn't you overextend by about nine hundred years?"

"Who me? Are you kidding, me make a mistake? Did you use the King James version or did you just go by the Sunday newspaper? Didn't you hear? Earth is going into the belt of light called, 'Photonic Field,' we're talkin' super-consciousness. I won't say when, but I'll give you a clue. The sun's corona enters the main on or about Fall Equinox of 1998, so I hope you enjoy roller coaster rides."

"Yep, sure do."

"Okay, good. Now this new energy field will extend human life to a capability of about a thousand Earth years, so have a nice heaven day.

"Now I'm gonna' go be all that is not for a couple of eternities if you'll sit in for me. I can use the tranquillity after this experience with you."

"Hey, what da' ya' mean by that?"

"Just kidding. Here take my throne."

"Wow! This is awesome. I'm actually in His… Oh, my God! I FEEL! I FEEL! ALL I FEEL IS LOVE! OH MY GOD! THAT'S ALL THERE IS! LOVE, ONLY LOVE! NOW I KNOW! I JUST KNOW! I KNOW EVERYTHING! ALL IS LOVE! JUST LOVE!

"Well, now 'I AM'! and know 'I AM'!, so I THINK I'll subdivide; let's say into a 100 trillion souls. I've got to share this feeling. This is awesome! I think I'll call it the process of evolution."

"Hey! Are you still with me?"

"Hah! Oh, what? WOW! We're still in the buggy? I just had this awesome daydream."

"No time for daydreaming. We got to get back for chow, we're keeping Mary and the gang. Hee ya! Giddyup there!"

All this to say: "Get a life and make it personal." Rather than focusing on what others should be doing with their lives or on what they think you should do with yours. Keep your mind focused on the inner winner, where the all that is, is always pressing out, desiring to be used.

The salvation of another or acceptance of it, is between them and one other, the only one. When you make it your business, you stand in judgment. Have no opinions of others. Be the example of ample to others by cultivating your own garden so you will have fruit to share instead of fertilizer to spread.

Live life deliberately, on purpose; your purpose, not by opinions of others. Be independent of what others think of you. Apply the psychology, "What others think of me is none of my business." Let Holy Spirit shine through you by acting whole. "Whole-I-Spirit."

Go within and touch the nature of the God source within your selfness, selfhood, self-worth, self-love, and become the solution to the problems rather than remaining the problem in need of solutions. You have so much to share of yourself if your focus is there. What do you have to share when your focus is on other's mistakes, failures or accomplishments? Look up the word "self" in your Webster. See for yourself the importance of this all-powerful word.

Become one of the meek and know the meaning of meek. I researched it. In my research, I would certainly say that they (the meek) fit the shoes of the "chosen few."

MEEK: Chooses love instead of war. Deserves Mother Earth because of their love for her. Submissive to the power of love. Stands back in wisdom and sends love to those who attack. Recognizes love as the source of all power. Unmotivated by ego. Slow to defend or justify. Evaluates others in a criterion of love rather than wealth, position, or situation. Like the wings of an eagle, stands fast in the storms of life. Warriors will pale in comparison to the meek one, for the power of one of these balanced ones is equal to legions of those without love.

Once you have fixed in your mind that you are on a volunteer mission from the Source, to co-create heaven on earth, you will not only be in on the viewing of auras, but so much more that is unperceived by your un-awakened faculties. There are not human words for the experience of senses that lie, yet un-awakened, within the being you already are.

Be meek with love, not weak with fear; the lowest of all vibrations one can reflect from is fear, which restricts the incoming thought to the lowest frequencies. To the exact degree of releasing of our fear-based attitudes, will the higher frequencies of love and light enter. The releasing of fear, in itself, opens and activates the somewhat dormant chakra system in your body which, in turn, channels new information to the DNA, overriding old programs.

HOW TO RELEASE FEAR 101

Step one: As it arises in its many faces, in consciousness, go directly to it and embrace it.

Step two: Ask it, "Why are you here?"

Step three: Ask it, "What can I learn from you?"

Step four: Bless it and thank it for coming to you.

Step five: Immerse it with divine love.

NEVER RESIST FEAR—or—just as the wild animal it is, it will know it can have you for its craving, jealousy, anger, hostility, hurry, worry, anguish, anxiety, frustration, melancholy, loneliness, depression, resentment, revenge, remorse. All associates of the negative nature have but one source. They originate from FEAR. Welcome this one with LOVE.

For those of you who believe fear is the enemy, good. The instructions were to love thine enemy, were they not?

"When one has love, they are no longer at the mercy of the forces greater than themselves, for they have become the great force."

May this great force be with you.

CHAPTER 21

ᘛhe ᑌltimate ᕈerception

*"If the doors to perception were cleansed,
everything would appear to man as it is...*

Infinite"

–William Blake

PERCEPTION:

Consciousness, observation, a mental image, physical sensation,
interpreted in the light of experience. Yes, I looked it up!

Once upon a sequence of times, there was a series of books
written. These books became the tools for many people
to become enlightened, for many enslavement, and for most
confusion.

For many others who read this series of books, the meanings in
them became a quest. Initially, these books were claimed to be inspired by some awesome, powerful stranger who seemed most illu-
sive, always in the mind of the advocate a mystical dude they mostly
called God, who lived somewhere else in a very distant land "place,"
called heaven. You certainly couldn't go there now—maybe later.
There was only ONE sure way to get there and by no other means

could this quest be accomplished.

During much of this time, in "the dark ages," hundreds and thousands were put to death if they did not believe in, and follow the commands or suggestions of what later became "THE BOOK."

Now get this humans, I wouldn't want to come on as a critic about the teachings inspired by some distant alien being who lives in a place far, far away, monitoring your every move and thought, but I will offer you a bit of wake-up challenge for the 90's that's 1990's AD.

As we move out of the dark ages into the Light of the "Photon Band," I feel it unnecessary to murder a man for doing so much work as rolling up his bed on the Sabbath, or a woman for baking bread on one particular special day of the week. So if only one day is holy, what are the other six? Back to war because your religion is right and the other wrong?

What puzzles me about this is the way in which humans accept "the leaders" now, as then, to opinionate "the book" to their meaning, so as to justify the right to murder others for such dastardly deeds as the baking of bread on church day.

Give me a break! Those days, these days—they are all the same days in the ultimate scheme of life. Just new and different experiences.

I deny not that there exists great spiritual truth and laws throughout the Bible, but if you do not discern it, others who have the attitude to control outside of themselves, like the ones who took it upon themselves to coerce, persuade, manipulate, and murder others out of minding the business of others, will use this particular "book" controversially to control you for selfish ends.

As the good, by the book, humans release the attitude of making you conform to what "they know" is right for "you," like as if they know your truth. Only then can they get to work on their own divine plan.

As we begin leading others with our example of nonjudgmental love, only then may we live our divine plan.

"Be ye lamps unto yourselves, be ye a refuge to yourselves.
Be taken yourselves to no external refuge."
–Buddha

"And be on guard against the good and the just!
They would crucify those who devise their own virtue."
–Nietzsche

God gifted us with freewill. How dare you take it away from another child of God. Just because someone doesn't speak the words, think the way, or act as you believe they should, you judge them as being unsaved—as if you are walking around on water showing the example of salvation.

Where in the cellular structure of your blood is the imagination of your mind when you are expressing the means of the way in which this titled by you, "Salvation" must occur? Have you ever studied more than one book on the subject? Well, have you?

Are you with the conviction that God gives this one prosperity and that one health, the other a handicap, and one poverty? Are you? Why? Does it not state in the book, "You choose your portion"?

Have you ever asked your inner being, Higher Self, in the center of you, "What is between me and a permanent state of joy?" Then sit in peace and be still for fifteen minutes and expect the answer may come from a person who guides you to a book, tape, show, idea, or circumstance.

It amazes me that some spend so much of their life preaching that you must get saved now, but you certainly cannot apply it yet, you must wait until you get somewhere else, not here, but somewhere up there, not now, but later. "They" keep you in the consciousness of waiting for later and you buy into it because they are a man of the Lord—yes, man—nearly always a man.

Yes, I am male species, but I abhor violence, war and external control. Women will graduate into the important offices as we ooze into the age called Aquarius which will shift this planet with a greater ease toward her new radiance. A quality that women have, for the most part, more so than men, their minds are on "open." Not intending categorization here, I certainly don't refer to the entire feminine species. I would like to see some female balance in the major religions.

The religious sector has imbedded in you, that you should go around trying to get others saved. This is to increase attendance at their church. However, before you assist in another's salvation, you need to qualify them as unsaved first, "judgment." Oh yeah, this be ascertained by them, with that ol' familiar question, "ARE YOU A CHRISTIAN?"

I've replied with many an answer to this question, but my favorite is, "Do you mean, am I one who follows or believes in the psychologies, teachings, and practices of the greatest mind scientist who ever walked the earth and one day will be same in Christ consciousness as He? Or do you mean, am I satisfied in just going around boasting to humans that I'm a Christian, but pretty sure I could never be Christ? Is it because of institutional conditioning you feel unworthy of claiming your Christhood in this moment? So when will you do it?" Will you wait until you "die"? Too late then, because in the "inner world" you'll know it for sure.

Religion is not what Jesus came to teach, but to un-teach or re-teach the practice of. Jesus was not religious, neither is His Father. At least not the orthodox meaning of the word. Don't you see? Yes, Jesus loved the church, but not what humans were doing within it.

If I have a choice to gather in a place that teaches me to duck the devil, evade evil and feel shame, or one that teaches the process of ascension, love, light, and life, I will certainly choose the latter.

The rules of the theological cemetery, I mean Seminary, will keep you immune to enlightenment and dead to your "I AM Christ Self," the very thing that intunes you to your own divinity. They teach more about evil and the work of the devil than of the process of salvation.

They tell you, "Don't follow astrology, it's the devils work." It's incredulous how influenced you are by one who thumps a book or wears a cross around his neck. God is not a book. He's a happening, through you, only when you allow. If you let your consciousness get asphyxiated on any "ism" or "ology," letting outside influences govern you, where is the flow of God (your feeling nature)? This is the same as "going by" any other institutionalized, structural system of beliefs.

The cross is symbolic of your divine self crossing the bridge out to the third dimension. When someone uses the cross as a reference to recall the most ridiculous murder of one certain individual that ever took place, they are in major misuse of it. Their purpose is control and manipulation. Astrology was initiated by GOD, Universal Source. You are astrological in your entire beingness. You are very related to those planets in our solar logos. "They each have their own glory," as do each of you. Those planets, my friends, happen to be your big brothers and sisters just as the ones you grew up with here. Here/there is only perception of separation in your minds. You are designed in the image of the very essence of those stars and planets. Know what you judge—or don't judge it.

Those beautiful planets are the creation of the Almighty Creator of the all that is and they, as He, loves you. Judgment equals anti-Christ, going away from light. When one assumes the other is unsaved, they have placed judgment upon another. Judgment is a disease held in the heart and causes heart disease.

Don't you see, if you are led to these truths, "THEY" (planetary control freaks) lose their organized, "under control" associated members, and attendance drops. Aren't you tired of being manipulated, controlled, and jerked around yet?

The clandestine elite or world management team have some of the very best salesMEN on earth. Selling you on the ideas that anything, but what they have, teach and believe, is, or could be, evil. Through "them" you will never know of the freedom that awaits you here and now, ON THIS BEAUTIFUL PLANET, because that would cost them another member. If you don't know you're in their psychological prison, you'll make no effort to escape. Will you? Have you? Do you know?

The most powerful of all their strongholds on you, is their psychology of eternal damnation in the burning pits of "hell fire," is it not? This is the most profound prefabricated line of BS they have left to hold you with.

Today if you're a law breaker you are sent to a correction facility or prison as we title it in our intellectual, linguistic terms. Normally this is on the outskirts of our cities now just as long ago. Hell was the name of the garbage dumps they used to send the nonconformists of past times to, away from the cities. That fire is going out soon because of the Aquarian Age that you are graduating into now. Aquarius is the Water Bearer and will assist in the dousing of their threats of everlasting fire for you to burn in.

Sure they can sell you on this idea. It's counterpart: separation, or the consciousness of, came with you as you entered the fetus and exited mama. Your memory was veiled, not to mention the umbilical cord of human babies is nearly always cut prematurely.

Every insight in this book is but a perspective of its title. Just as every experience in your life has come to nudge you, to remind you of who you are. This body I live in and focus through is the human extension of who I really am, my experiential vehicle.

There is but one thing and only one thing eternal and that is the only thing that is. Most call it God and that's okay as long as you don't psychoanalyze it as "separate." The more proper terms, if you must apply title, are life, light, love, or source, or if you would like it directly from the words in "the book," in the words Jesus spoke, "Tell them I AM sent me." So who is God? Where does God live? Who does God live through? Who sent you, someone else?

As long as they can keep you in fear, confused, and defused, rather than the more proper methods Jesus taught of direct co-fusing with the Father, Source within, they can maintain their careers in mass control and serve their selfish ends. They have kept you in a state of organized denial in protection of their own job security.

There is no death. There is not but life, everlasting life. Life eternal in the Light. Whether you see it from your level of shutdown, closed-up limitations that you continue to hold your "self" victim to or not. The Light is, always was, and always will be there. All you have to do is open your mind and turn on to it. There is no death, there is only everlasting life (now-moment life) forever and ever. Give yourself daily wake-up calls, instructions to God and His mighty hierarchy of your intents and acceptance of His light. No one else can make this call for you.

"Beloved ascended masters illumine my consciousness
in the light of the cosmic Christ."

When someone turns out the light in your room, does it mean the light is not there or that you just don't see it? No matter how long it has been out, when you turn on to it, you shine. Step into the light by simply setting your focus of attention away from human discord and onto the energy that beats your heart. "Turn cheek"!

Like our sun, this "great central sun" within is always turned on. You are the one who turns it off by your attention toward other gods, so to speak (discord). Our planet or clouds may come between you and our sun but it does not quit shinning because of a cloudy day.

The clouds are your attention to human fears/discord. Make the switch to pure, positive, source energy. Select joy for all your experiences here. Stop focusing on the clouds (human discord). Start focusing on the sun (joy).

Some of you have a favorite verse, John 3:16. Your personal salvation, right? Why? Because it gives you reassurance that the fella' you call God didn't leave you behind out here in this mess, right? You say you must be born again, cleansed in the blood, baptized in water and Spirit and accept "The Lord Jesus Christ" as your personal savior and that is your passport to freedom, home, heaven, right? Of course, you can back this all up, I mean it's in "the book," right?

Yes, in a very limited understanding of the process, you are right. Now listen as I share a grand perception, to increase your level of awareness and expansion.

The word baptism; the erasing power of the mind—it's not a one-time dunking process, it's a mental reconditioning process. The word repent; change the mind. Of course, you must change the mind and recondition it from all the notions of controlism stimulated by the world management team, or whatever conditionalized you.

The organizations of any title that teach their way is truth, also teach you in an ever-so-sly way that they have the answers. NOW LET'S GET OUR ATTENDANCE UP FOR NEXT SUNDAY! Wake-up time is here or this blasphemy, as many control artists will label it, could not be in print. Why do they want more attendance? If you truly wish to know, do the unspeakable. Ask them if you, as a financier of their nonprofit organization, may bring your accountant in for a little book review of all their books, not just the black one being thumped on Sunday. Non-profit, my ass! It's all about money and power—something up to now "they" have plenty of.

About thirty years after the year zero when the brave one grew up; He one day entered the temple and became down right pissed off because of the money changers there, right? Wrong, just another cover up. The administrators were charging for prayers, baptism, and salvation. Jesus did not come to 3-D to teach you to go to the church and condemn you if you don't. He came to teach you to go direct to Source, as did He, with no middle man to collect on your way.

The word church means; to gather, not to support ritual. If there is a place you enjoy going to gather, do it, of course. A church needs your financial support to pay rent, but keep in consciousness that the 10% of giving of self is a universal law set forth as to insure your receiving. You must stay generous in order to generate, therefore, create. "I CAME THAT THEY MAY HAVE LIFE AND HAVE IT MORE ABUNDANTLY."

This 10% law was twisted from its original purpose for you and your pocket, to them and their pocket. This law was set even before the Old Testament. Read *The Richest Man In Babalon* for confirmation on this. The law of gold or money is that you give yourself 10% of all you earn and the next law is that you invest it so it has children—interest—and its children have children—compound interest.

All spiritual metaphysicians know that the body and blood of Jesus were purified and that each cell was energized with original spiritual substance and life, until all materiality was purged away and only pure essence remained. This essence was sown as seed in the whole race consciousness. Whosoever, through faith in Christ, draws to self one of these life germs, becomes inoculated to that degree with Christ consciousness, and not only the mind, but also the body is cleansed.

Likened unto a healing process, hah? Here's another grand perception.

Thousands of our years ago, there was an alteration of our deoxyribonucleic acid; which to the ones performing this ungodly deed, seemed the best way of gaining planetary control over the human race.

When Jesus came this was His ultimate purpose, to correct, in our blood stream, that which had been lost or altered. The most prominent and aggressive of all cover-ups about this man Jesus was this: He was successful on His mission, yes, but unlike many believe, it was not His death that saved us, but the inoculation of our blood stream. This was accomplished through none other than Mary Magdalene. Among other things, she is a Goddess and Jesus' twin flame. Oh, you need not take my word for something so revealing, it's in "the book." She is in there twelve times, Matthew through John, and each time she's lookin' for her man.

If this information leaked out, that Jesus succeeded in his mission, the Gods, Kings, clandestine elite, world management team, and/or whomever had the desire to play control freak over us would have lost their flock, us.

As we regain our natural position as the whole "I" Spirit, "I AM" Christ, God "I AM" personified and expressed through the body, we will realize that we need not exterior guidance for salvation, but internal re-veil-ation only. By the way, as long as you don't believe it, you're right, again!

That's one of the strange paradoxes of the third dimension. You have the right to believe any way you choose. Any way you believe is right for you; therefore, your truth. Any way you can believe this— that it is, in fact, through the blood of Jesus that you may obtain illumination, that covers all the salvation's; physical, mental, spiritual, emotional, financial, social, and family.

Oh, by the way, if you look up the word deoxyribonucleic acid, it will say DNA or vice versa. If you look up RNA, it will say, "See DNA." Yes, it was our DNA, molecules, "they" tampered with and now our scientific laboratories are up to the level of knowledge about our molecules that they, too, have the knowing of how to manipulate us through them. However, not to FEAR, that's the ingredient that gives them power.

This beautiful planet, and all upon her, are just about to go through the null zone of the Photon Belt and once again, we regain our own personal God powers; to create, preserve, and transform.

Of course, if you would desire to carry on in 3-D awareness and remain in this limitedness, you have the freewill and limitless time to do so. There should be plenty of people to help guide you with all their belief systems, to assist you "for your own good," to remain in your limits.

The mandatory ingredient of opposite polarity to fear, needed to sustain the vibrations necessary for transformation from 3-D survival to 5-D ecstasy, is LOVE. Yes, the meek shall inherit this gorgeous ol' girl all right, not to confuse meek with weak. For a quick, easy reference, on the meaning of meek, use Jesus as an example; the awesome power of Divine Love.

At this point in these teachings I will insert the picture that tells a thousand words.

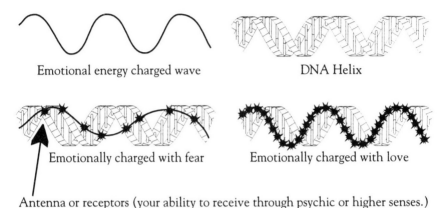

Emotional energy charged wave   DNA Helix

Emotionally charged with fear   Emotionally charged with love

Antenna or receptors (your ability to receive through psychic or higher senses.)

For you who have scientific knowledge in this field of study, this is certainly not to impress you with my non-formal information of same.

My desire here is to place an idea of how the emotional body and activities of the mind may cause an opening or shut down to your natural creative powers according to the way in which you express your energies. If you require more specific education on the scientific theory of the inner workings of your molecules, there are many books on the subject.

And for the humans who think this story of the alteration of our DNA sounds unrealistic, I'm with ya'. But then, is all that you sense through your five senses reality, or real-to-you? Seems so but how could your physical body be real if you die? If it's not permanent, how could it be real? If it's not eternal, it possesses not the quality we phrase as reality. Your five senses are only a temporary extension of their creator, the real you. All that you sense through them is just the illusions you create for, let's say, recreational purpose—third dimension/Maya/illusion. However, while you're in it, what will you put on your screen in your next role to play? What will you download into your molecules in your very next opportunity? Which is now.

Whatever it may be, if it is placed there in a vibratory state of joy, it will be well received.

People often ask me if I'm psychic. I don't affirm or deny it. I often reply, "I am in the vibration of love."

If you desire the higher vibrations of living, it is you that must place yourself in them. You must step forth in determined command over your emotional body without wavering. Never again let it sense a weakness in your dominion over it.

If you wish to live the life-style of mastery, you must master your style of life. Your life-style is governed by your feeling nature.

You may have no discord to be master—none—not even mild dislike.

HEIGHTENING YOUR PERCEPTIONS:

You may not change the world, but there is always one thing changeable in yours, and that is your perception to the world around you. I refer to you, the first person, the personal self. Know this self person. The most loving person is self-centered. Jesus, the individual man, was very self-centered.

Now, I'll give you a few words here that should supply enough time, as you read them, to see what I'm gonna' say next for you to place judgment on. Okay, now, have you tried walking on water lately or multiplying your meal to feed a thousand times more people than you cooked for? You couldn't sway me to believe that guy was not centered within Himself, so centered, that He knew what all the different selves were feeling, thinking, and experiencing at the same time

You are an individual self on many planes or dimensions of existence. Jesus spoke of these different areas of life. "I go and prepare for your return into higher consciousness, "mansions," as he termed it.

If you look in your Webster under "self," you will find it followed by different words almost four hundred times. You must become self-centered if you wish to recondition your self. You must be independent of the opinions of others. "What others think of me is none of my business."

Your life is mostly the way it is now, conditioned by six ingredients and all six are contagious to each other; your thoughts, your words, your actions, other's thoughts, words, and actions. Change any one of the first three and the other two will follow along. But how do you change the last three?

Silly rabbit tricks are for magicians. You've been trying to change others all your life and look where it has gotten you—right out of your own personal power of the possibility of changing self, the one and only person on this planet changeable by you.

Your words have tremendous power. Be selective with them or don't speak. As you speak negative words, you continue to set up lower vibrations in the cellular structure YOU live in. How can you atone to the higher states of awareness if you continue to drag the body down with these poisons? Know that it is the intent or meaning behind the word that carries the vibration.

The same holds true to the reaction of someone who attaches negative meaning to something like a crystal. I've witnessed people react, like Clark Kent would to Kryptonite, when someone whips out a crystal—even though they wear one on their arm to keep perfect time and track the aging process (their watch).

Stop trying to please these people who base their lives on fear. Don't think you must sacrifice your *self* to be loved. Don't go around trying to please others; be pleasant, yes.

It is your feelings that you should let guide you. Feeling is the communication of the spirit. God's li'l messengers. The part of you most obvious to yourself, is your physical self, your body. There is more to you than meets the retina. You are also an emotional body, or mess, whichever the case may be. Your emotions or emotional body is, in fact, your advisory board, E-motion, energy in motion. It is not the enemy, nor will it hurt you. It is you, one of you. God's most powerful messenger is experience.

As you continue to experience emotions/feelings that you allow to affect you negatively, like loneliness, emptiness, anger, depression; and you are well aware that the list goes on; know that the whole list, all of it, comes from one, and only one base, FEAR. There isn't a negativity that is not supplied by fear, the grandfather of all evil. It is not the word, action, deed, or thought that dis-eases you, but your personal reaction to it.

Which are you choosing today? What is your vibrational offering to your universe (source-energy)?

F alse	**L** et
E vidence	**O** thers
A ppearing	**V** isions
R eal	**E** xist

– *OR* –

H allucinations	**H** ighest
E xemplified	**E** nergy
L acking	**A** nd
L ove	**V** ibrational
	E xperience
	N egotiable

– *OR* –

STORY TIME:

Buddha was walking down the road one day. There was a fella' who had heard of him and his ways, so he set out to test him. As he met up with Buddha on the road, he began calling him degrading, slanderous names; casting aspersions that the Buddha is evil and does the work of the devil.

He said, "You'll go to hell and burn forever in the pits of eternal damnation."

The fella' spit at Buddha and continued to condemn him. Finally after all the attempts to rile the Buddha failed, the fella' stopped Buddha in the path and said, "I heard about you. You think you're some kinda' God or something. You go around living in peace and harmony while the rest of us, out here in the 'real world,' work for a livin' and fight for what we believe in, but not you, you think you can just breeze through this thing called life. So now let me ask you, how on earth do you go around being some kind of guru with all this crap going on out here?"

The Buddha looked into the eyes of the fella' with a calm, loving gentleness and said, "May I ask you a question?"

The fella' replied," "Well sure, go ahead."

Buddha asked, "If you offer a man a gift and the man does not accept the gift, to whom then does the gift belong?"

To this, the fella' replied, "Well, if the other guy doesn't want it, I get to keep it anyway, so it'd be mine."

Buddha said, "I don't accept your gift," and continued walking merrily down the path. Alikened unto the teapot that sings merrily, even though it's up to its neck in hot water. The soaring eagle has no need to be appreciated by ground creatures.

What is your perception of your life? "It's hell out here?" or "It's heaven in here." The choice lies in the gifts you accept, does it not? What is your perception of life? Is it happening to you through you, or is it caused by you?

Fear, lack, want and limitation is ample in the psychology of the world's thinking. You may live upon this beautiful planet without partaking of its ugly human thinking. "Be not of the world" (human thoughts). "Cast down your worldly possessions" (attitudes based in fear), not your Toyota. BE INDEPENDENT OF THE OPINION OF OTHERS!

The high mind, "Let that mind be in you," comes from within, not from without. As we climb back up to integrity of soul purpose, our understanding increases and our social life may decrease.

Our selfish little pity parties cease. What we pity, anyway, is altered self/alter ego because it's about to lose its residence of stay. It thrives on things like self-pity. Once you begin to *be*, rather than follow the organized methods of *not to be*, the question becomes the answer, "To thine own higher self be centered." The truth is a very serious threat to misery. If you had two choices in a Spielberg movie role, your first ever, to play the role of a beggar or a king/queen, which would you choose?

Know this entity, whatever the role of life you are now in, you—soul of your selves—chose. If you no longer desire to play the role, don't ask a stranger in a far away land to fix it for you, change it! Story time again.

I met a fella' one time who told me he went into a cave in the foothills of California for forty days, in deep meditation. He said he asked the universe why life is so mucked up. He got a definite reply, "IF YOU DON'T LIKE IT, CHANGE IT!" Kind of a hint of who's in charge, hah?

To change your life, in any way, you will find it most helpful, first to know the part you desire changed.

First of all, how not to make a change. Change cannot occur with a closed mind. Whatever it is you prefer to change, do not resist it any longer. What you continue to resist will continue to persist.

Major example: If you seek change in a relationship, you must, first and foremost, release anything you've been resisting. Allowance is the key here. If someone's gift is not acceptable to you, good. Don't accept the gift or play into the role, but do, by all means, allow. God allows everything, so who might you be to dis-allow anything? But then, God is smarter than the average bearer of his light. All great discoveries have been made from a willingness to NOT BE RIGHT! If you have that all-so-common dis-ease, "The need-to-be-right syndrome," ask yourself where it has gotten you so far.

Next step, love is not conditional. Was it your well-meaning parents who non-consciously taught you that love is conditional. Let me ask you a question I have been eager to ask the world ever since I first began to make the discovery of more than just an ol' phrase "unconditional love." Do you live life as it is, or are you trying to get someone to see it your way?

As I began to un-condition the standards I felt or demanded others should live up to, my attitude of manipulate and control began to subside. My self-imposed prison doors began to rattle loose. I began to rise above a condition that I didn't have the foggiest idea I was causing. My relationships with others began to change incredulously. I found that I was miserably married because someone else decreed that I stay married till death do us part. What is most important to you in a relationship, longevity, or quality?

Well, after considering death rather than marriage, I got to doing a li'l figurin' and it dawned on me—grand perception here. It's not the marriage I'm in, it's the reason I'm in it; I needed someone to fill a gap. I needed someone to go places with, needed regular sex, needed someone's outside support, needed pity, and, get this one, felt the need to settle down and grow up. Should you get married to have children, or have children to get married? If you have children, should you get married? "Whoops, I got pregnant, so I better get married." Excellent reasons to commit? I think not!

If you go for the idea that is emphasized almost exclusively by the male species, normally pastors, that God put all marriages together and you're stuck in it till death-do-you part, examine this conversation.

On a radio program, March 12, 1997, I heard this: "I'm, so-and-so, on the so-and-so, program. What's your question?"

"This is Sara _____. I haven't been going to church for over a year so I know I'm not saved anymore, but I just want advice on my marriage. My husband goes out drinking and stays out all night at times. He has come in many times and beat me up. He has abused me physically, mentally, and emotionally. He has also abused the children. What do you recommend I do?"

"There is only one thing you can do, by God's law, and that's submit to him, no matter what, and be obedient. Love him and try to bring him to the Lord and get him saved."

This was near the end of the program so they didn't say much more, but I turned it off anyway. Let me ask you. Do you see something wrong with this picture?

I thought I had switched to a program replay from the dark ages. If your spouse should ever strike you, one time, you need to do two things; ONE, ask your mighty "I AM" Presence why. Then, TWO, immediately release yourself from them. Male or female, never submit yourself to hostility. Forgive it and leave, or kick them out, whichever can be done by the break of day. I couldn't believe this man told that lady to obey that! Then get him "saved," believing herself not to be, because she hasn't attended church for a time. When you hear people speaking in this way, it may help if you could just splash some cold water on them.

Here's another grand perception. I personally believe that to re-
kindle an old flame that still burns is okay. However, I don't believe
kicking a dead horse is gonna' get him back up. Why continue to
deny your feelings?

When it's over, the feelings of your higher self lets you know
through your vehicle called heart-center. By no spiritual or universal laws are you bound to a being because you signed a paper, gave a
ring, made a commitment, or a baby. About this latter part, I won't
delve into it here, but let me express one concept about abortion.

You may kill a living fetus, but you will never kill a living soul. In
most cases, the soul enters the baby as it begins its travel out of the
birth canal into the earth's atmosphere. Let me say, on behalf of your
pithy judgments onto the woman who chooses to abort. If you don't
trust her with a choice, how can you trust her with a child?

I'll go on to say, if you are the one CONTROLLING the situation and prevent the abortion, you've just taken total responsibility
to see to it that the child has everything it needs till it severs from
home. Even if she should place the child in your home. Did you not
"make up" her mind for her, therefore purchase the responsibility for
the child? If you manipulate the incarnation into being, you should
damn sure be there to support the incarnated.

Back to marriage, if you are in one that sucks, get out and get into
another one that sucks whether it's with a contract or not, it's still
marriage when you shack up. Let me explain, it's not "the marriage"
that sucks, it's what you are not facing about yourself. Until you
arrive at the realization that your spouse or partner is reflecting you,

you may continue to go from one to the next with the most preva-lent appearance. They suck! Marriage is a reflection of you. Just like people who smoke, people don't really smoke, except maybe some-one who overloads their crack pipe. I won't mention Richard's name here, but if you see someone smoking, call 911. They've got a prob-lem. It's the cigarette that smokes, the person is the sucker. Now, I'm not saying cigarettes smoke and people suck, or marriages suck. I *am* implying *attitudes* and only one—YOURS.

There is, in fact, only one problem in your life and that's YOU, not someone else, somewhere else. If you want a fix, no one is gonna' do it for you. How will you ever become the master of your life, if you believe someone else can master it for you?

If you think God will do it for you, then this may come as a shock to you, but she won't. She will supply your every need to remake your life as desired and you must ask for her assistance. Source doesn't play favoritism to anyone or thing. Source does not control, ma-nipulate, or persuade. Source just is. Source is not biased and does not judge or discriminate. Source knows you by the vibrations you produce.

At review time when you leave your physical body, you will judge yourself and no other will stand in your judgment but you. Judgment Day is today and at the end of today, it's today again, and one day it will be one of your cycles of completion. At the end of this lifetime as you know it, and for you, it will be today. Your today is the only day you will ever be aware of. The eternal NOW. Yes, you are right smack dab in the center of eternity NOW! I hope you are comfort-able, it's where you've always been and where you always will be, in the eternal NOW.

So now that you know when the time is to make changes, we can go on. Feelings, as they come to you DURING THE EXPERIENCE of having them, is the only time you have to make the perception switch. As said before, I'll remind you, it makes no difference how long your light has been out, when you switch it on, you shine.

View these "feelings" as God's li'l messengers, and be advised that not every reaction to them is from Central Source. How could there be growth without contrast, therefore the need of discernment? Until you make atonement with each and everyone of your feelings, they will be back to haunt you rather than guide you. The choice is up to you, whether to refute them or embrace them. As long as you resist, they persist. Even after you've made atonement (at-one-ment) with them, you will know them, but in a new light, a new perception. They become your guides and li'l loved ones.

The time you must challenge yourself and your feeling is at the very depth, point, happening of fear, anger, loneliness, depression, emptiness, anxiety, or any of fear's relatives. Ask it to identify itself. Ask, "Why have you come to me?" Then ask, "What can I learn from you?" Then say, "Thank you for guiding me. Bless you, I love you divinely." You may need to apply this to many different feelings, but it won't take many times for each. Feelings, in themselves, are from the divine. They are, in fact, perfect. It's our frame of reference that has marred a clear reception of them.

It's this awesome power of love that transcends your experience of the emotion. Once applied, you will have your own proof. If any tend to linger, causing pain in any part of your body, notice which part of your body pains. Focus there and with great respect, ask these energies to release themselves and return to their homes. Smudging or burning incense is very helpful here.

It's not getting "rid of" here we're talkin', it's transformation by atonement. We have been going through life after life attempting to dump, get rid of, release, relinquish, avoid, and resist one of us, one of our bodies, our emotional body, our own personal advisory board. We dodge it, hide from it, curse it. No wonder it keeps after us like a li'l lost puppy dog you keep feeding. What formula do we apply to get rid of or away from these nasty li'l negative reactions to our feelings?

We use the same ingredient that negative reaction feeds on— hate. We hate it when this or that happens, but how about using its opposite polarity—love. No-o-o-o, because you just hate it when someone else is right, right? We hate it when someone gets hostile.

We hate it when they don't understand us. It even pisses us off when we get angry. When the child acts selfish, we take away the child's toys. What a reinforcement that is.

When we feel lonely, we give ourselves a pity-party. The boss threatens to fire you and you bow in fear of loss. Someone flips you off, you flip back, twist it, and scream, "More of it to you, Buddy." I always found that to be an interesting choice of titles for one's enemy.

The biggest paradox of all—condemnation. You are attempting to fix, build or repair something that you know you should have taken to the shop, or called the ones who make their living doing it right. But no-o-o-o, you have a do-it-yourself manual that cost you more time trying to understand than the repair was worth. As you broke the stud off way down in the block, got stuck up in the vent sucking poisonous soot, bent the hell out of the new screen that you finally purchased for the kid's window, used the wrong tool for the job and pinch your finger, OOW! What do you call in for reinforcement? A DAMN!

You ask the Almighty power of the Universe, God Himself, to damn what you are trying to bless. This is all about you! Your relationship to all upon this planet. You are doomed to repeat the same basic roles in all your relationships, to include the ones you have with the tools that you fix things with, and the chair that you sit in, until you realize that all of it is your mirror.

Your feelings, denied, will return with new and more profound ways of getting you to recognize yourself through them until you do; life, after life, after life. Why so much stress on relationships? Because that's all you have to view you by. You are the link in the theory of relativity. You are the relationship to all consciousness around you. So, if there is no consciousness around you, you are not! You would then be nothing/ no-thing. No-thing to relate to, you are not relative. When Ralph told Alice he's the boss and she's nothing, Alice had quite a point when she told Ralph, "Well Ralph, I guess that means you're the boss of nothing." It's the content (conditioning) in the bread (mind) that determines whether or not it raises, not the oven.

Your best teachers in life often have the worst attitudes. Be receptive that every contact is the soul's contract and reveals something new about yourself. Voluntarily fail until you realize it's only a word.

Love the uncomfortable. Allow crisis to shake you until you can receive it as a neutral observer. If you resist, argue, defend, deny, or already "know that," how can the teacher give to you? The most profound of all teachers, those you dodge the most— your feelings. When you know loss is not loss, but change, you can live the miracle of true reality and joy. "Empty yourself of yourself," the little ego-self. Let the mind be silent and flow with events. A certain sign of gaining understanding is when you no longer criticize troublesome people, but feel empathy toward them. Drop the "want-to-be-right attitude."

Grand perception: The pain lies between what you think should happen and what actually happens. If our demand for things to happen is relinquished, the pain gap vanishes.

Release old ridiculous laws, rules, traditions, and patterns that are not growth-oriented. Your opportunity to experience the new awaits you, but new experience cannot happen without change. Change is not accepted without an open mind. If the "I AM" Presence within you is gonna' enjoy the ride through what we term *life*, it is evolution that takes you there. How can evolution continue if the vehicle for its process is shut down, closed minds? Start planting new seeds in your garden (mind), in tonight's meditations and grow a new crop, circumstances, and understanding of them in your life.

Clean up your defamation's like, "It's hard," "That's impossible," "I can't," to affirmations like, "I AM." If you're confused or upset and not sure what to say, just walk around saying, "I AM!," "I AM!," "I AM!"

As long as you continue to burden yourself with the preconditioned fear-provoking sermons gifted to you by sometimes well-meaning individuals, structured by organizations that want to control whomever and whatever they can, you will not get it!

As long as you live by belief systems, rather than your own feelings within, you will not get it! The verse is, "Have dominion over the planet," not your brothers and sisters that are here with you. The first, last, and only problem you will ever have in your relationships with any one, place, or thing, is your own setting of any condition. JUST ONE! Bet you can't set just one.

You've all heard the term "reverse psychology." Have you heard of the psychology of diverting their attention? Instead of reading the side of the bag that states, "8-12 grams, 12-24% of your daily required fat content in about twelve chips" and making a decision based on that information, you stuff 200%-500% of the fat your body needs and get sick afterwards. It's not like the chips don't already have enough going for them, they taste GREAT!

They run ads for one purpose, more greenback, $$$$, the answer to all 3-D things. Those are your thoughts, right? Another lure to keep you here. Until you "GET IT" you will remain out here. You will continue to judge it, and as long as you judge it, you assure yourself one more round of this limitation in your next 3-D life, again, and again.

When you judge yourself to be saved and someone else not to be saved, that's judgment. It is unto you, as you judge it unto them. Judgment equals anti-Christ, headed away rather than toward your "I AM" Christ self. If you judge one to be unsaved, if I read the bible correctly, this would indicate by that placement of judgement you are unsaved.

There will be judgment, as this book hits the marketplace. I've been told that I've been preparing for this over eons of time. Astrologically it has been shown to me that I have come before "my time" and boy do I believe it. Unexpectedly, even by the angelic host, the company of heaven has been allowed entrance into our lower dimensions. It has truly become time for many to return to the Garden of Paradise.

Allow the stimuli of this, and many books like it, to activate your higher God centers. Know that these are your tools, you are the power. *Later* is only a *now* you haven't yet experienced. The reason *later* never happens to you is because you are always in the eternal *now*. Salvation is now, not later, thank God.

If you elevate your teachers to a pedestal in your mind, you step out of your point of personal power. You have experienced eons of preparation for your purpose. Out here on 3-D, I am looking just as you for something more real. However, I no longer look "out there." I go within daily and will continue till I am within the awareness of my higher mind facilities, THE ALMIGHTY "I AM" PRESENCE in full waking consciousness. I have discovered that going within is not optional, if you wish to arrive where we all truly wish to. Going within is the sure cure for going without. Read everything, but read it with discernment.

There is a concept in one of the metaphysical books expressing a method of replacing the guidance assigned to you. Within the readings, it is explained how you may summon, in the darkness, a new set of guides through what is titled, "The Neutral Implant." I understand that even members of the United Nations have submitted to this idea. They also claim that you cannot undo it once done. Could that be so you won't try?

If you happen to be one who summoned these "new guides" and it worked, you may have gathered a lot of new li'l friends in your head and find it quite busy up there. You may also find your body in your local holding facility with a straight jacket around it. If it didn't work for you, it's not luck. It's your higher spiritual atonement of light that protected you from your little self, alter ego. That li'l devil's always gettin' into mischief.

Whenever you do meditations or spiritual work of any kind, surround yourself in the light. You may keep it simple, but do it.

Now here's how you release those pesky li'l demons that may have cost you your marriage, career, family, car, friends; basically your life.

"From the Lord God of my being, I call forth the mighty "I AM" Presence and the all consuming violet fire to release me from all elementals and entities that are not of Divine Love and Light. Bless you. With respect, I command that you return to your homes. In the name of divine love, thank you."

I have come to bring forth this message to my race, my dearly beloved brothers and sisters, all of you of the Human Race. For he/she that hath an ear, let the sound of divinity ring in your minds. As you fall off to sleep, verbally, or mentally recite these words, Divine Love. Then begin to spell them out D-I-V-I-N-E L-O-V-E over and over. Be your own test for their effect on you. Have a note pad ready for recording dreams they invoke. If you don't recall your dreams, just spell it out ten to twenty times before bed, verbally D-R-E-A-M-S.

In brief, here's a simple way of visualizing in your mind's eye a picture of what is happening on and within our planet from a greater, grander, wider viewing point.

OUR SOLAR SYSTEM MOVING INTO THE PHOTON BELT

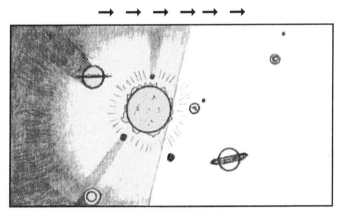

OUR SUN ENTERS THE PHOTON BELT ON OR ABOUT SEPTEMBER 23, 1998

The "Goddess Mother Earth" is coming out of her cocoon, her adolescence. No more a virgin to the love source energies. The loving light of the universal cosmos has been in foreplay long enough. Earth is being made love to by Source. More specifically, entering the band of light called "Photon Belt." She is undergoing the experience of cosmic orgasm. Climax is near. The ones in love with her and all upon her will enjoy this vibration with her. The ones who won't be joining us and her are not likely reading this book, especially this deep into it.

If you are not fixed in the vibration of love, as we get deep enough into the Photon Belt/Band, you will not inherit the earth. We, our solar system, will arrive near halfway into this magnificent band of Photonic Light particles in our year 1998, around mid-Fall. When our Sun goes in deep enough, that's called the null zone.

The protonic energy that we now use will all be canceled out for three days. Yes, the sky will become darkened. No big deal, stay where you are, light your candles, and after the third day of dark, there will be about two days of light; too much light, to view with your eyes. Either have welder's glasses or stay inside. The rest to know is within your nature.

We will be in this light for 2,000 years again, then back to the dark ages for another 11,000 years. This is the opportunity for many who have been here, in most cases hundreds of lifetimes, to illuminate out of the 3-D entrapment where any God can come along and assert control over you. Stay tuned for more perception/correction.

From 1998 through 2012, the most major shifts ever known to hu-man, planetarily and consciously, will take place. If you wish not to be left behind, AGAIN, do as the masters say and do. "Awaken that in you that sleepeth." Your "third eye" which is the pituitary gland and pineal body in the center of your head. In your meditations connect your heart, head, and throat.

As long as you confuse Jesus, the man, with the power source that came to Him and through Him, you will not GET IT! Jesus named it his "Father" that doeth the work. We then, as now, looked to the personality Jesus as He stood and said, "All these works you will do."

We saw the power He used that is available to us and thought, "He sure is special."

As He attempted to express between stone throwing, "You are all of the most high."

We focused on Him instead of Source within. That's why, at one time, he said (to paraphrase), I'm outta' here dudes/dudettes, you're still not gettin' the message. Or, "It is expedient that I go away, for if I do not go, the Comforter will not come," The "I AM" Christ consciousness.

Here comes another grand perception: There be several till we get to the ultimate, a'?

Armageddon is an indoor activity in the consciousness of your mind-body. How mankind handles those locusts will determine exactly how the outer role of Armageddon affects us and our planet. Armageddon can be "the Harmonic Convergence," but not likely, by the looks of traffic, the way eartheans act in it. Traffic seems to me the simplest way to gauge the reaction levels of humans. How do you react or respond in it? That is your bro/sis on your bumper.

Here's another grand perception; crystal, magnifying power source. Christ All, magnifying power source. This *Christ activity* is what activates through the crystalizing or magnifying properties of the "Third Eye" or pineal/pituitary glands, center of your brain.

The "I AM" Christ, of you, is stationary; just above and at the top center of your head. Its conduit is the crown chakra atop the head. Its magnifiers are of crystal tissue within the pineal body, in the center of the head and the pituitary gland, just in front of the pineal. As one merely focuses their attention on these areas, they begin to activate just as the dry leaf begins to sizzle as you position the magnifying glass between the sun and about a foot above the leaf. The power source is within and above the head. Its name is *Light*. "The light, energy source of the body is the eye, pituitary gland. If, therefore, thine eye be single, focused on through meditation, thy whole body shall be full of light, illuminated."

The manifesting source from within your vehicle, body, temple is centralized at the center of your brain, pineal body, seat of the soul, from whence it flows forth into the pituitary gland, distribution center of personality. If you concentrate on light flowing into and through these two glands, connecting them, as they bond, merge, and connect the will of your higher mind (soul) is accepted into your personality, pituitary gland, alter ego, and contemplation, soul doing the thinking, is acquired. Simply put, when you give way to the higher feelings or will within the organs of your body, this leads to the activation of your higher mind within doing the thinking called contemplation. The little-man ego is placed permanently on override.

Illumination takes place, soul takes over, you go to heaven and never even leave the farm. More accurately, you brought the consciousness of heaven life or higher dimension unto your awareness. "It is appointed unto alter ego to die but once." This is that process. Believe it or else, you'll be back. "Seek ye first the kingdom," crown chakra, opening.

Once upon a time there was an entity who, as he arrived at his own personal Godlike powers, took dominion over certain areas at their weak points in time and played the role of major "control freak" and manifested great fear among the people there, US! NOW! I'm a brave kinda' guy, but stupid is as stupid does, right? So I don't put myself in that category, I won't be printing the name of this entity or god, because in other dimensions, it still manifests and manipulates.

This has not to do with a fear of this powerful being, but a heightened level of awareness I have succumbed to through my own personal experiences and research work.

This god-being demanded that humans give him all respect and even sacrifice life for his games. It is said that out of anger or play, he would strike humans down with electrical currents, enough to fry them. That doesn't scare me about the big dodo head either, but here's why I do not name his well-known title.

There are still millions of earthlings under his rule. At their hands, many have hung till death on a cross or been beheaded, stoned, beaten, and cast out of the societies, under thumb of this self-elected god-being. Although he's lost his interest now in playing us as his puppets, the impressions left run deep in our cellular codes, so there are still masses of followers out to get you if you don't conform, if you don't pay allegiance to this god who totally convinced them that he is the most high living God or Universal Source. God, the omni present, Universal Source, cosmic consciousness of all that is, was, and ever will be. The ALL is always there for all to use, no matter how they decide to use it. In other words, you too can manipulate others in a major way when you come to your major powers, but then the universe will repay, the same way you convey.

Some of the manipulation from this other entity came down through many of our world popular organizations that teach you to give your life over to, and here they place a title, then you wait. Wait for salvation later, maybe? Wait for those pearly gates later, heaven later, God later, Christ later, illumination later, after you have lived. Then you go to heaven, later! They say come forward "now," key word here, stay up with me, that part, the NOW part, is a truth. Then give your life to someone, somewhere else as it was taught in the Piscean Age. They, the males in control, teach it's a dude, not a dudette, that you give personal self to, but the truth is the energy, known as God, is androgynous, includes both polarities.

Grand perception next: As soon as you remember who you really are, you can become whomever you would really like to be. As we remember our multi-dimensionality, the Christ will awaken within us because it is time.

There is really only one dis-advantage you have. There are many dis-ease-ments going around our planet, through her human, alleged "caretakers." Dis-appointment fuels dis-couragement, from which emerges dis-stress, bringing dis-comfort, igniting dis-cord that creates dis-sonance, that begets dis-satisfaction, causing dis-harmony, making dis-tortion, leading to dis-agreement, feeding dis-trust, the forebear of dis-aster. All be-caused by one DIS; dis-connection with Source.

As long as you continue to go for the BS, THEY, outside-of-you forces, condition you with: "You won't get the message here." You will continue to empower THEM, to keep you unconscious of, or dis-associated with Source—the one and only true, what most title God, LIGHT, your high personal self. How do you reconnect with Source? Embrace it! ALL of it! It is ALL! Do you fear yourself? Embrace each and everything that happens in your life. You see, when fear has you on the run, it's got you on its hook. That's why you are still out here. DO NOT RESIST IT. THAT FEEDS IT!

By law of attraction, you attract what you fear. Fear, anger, resentment, depression, etc., are not the enemy, they are the entities that bring messages to you, your messiahs they are. Messiah, I looked it up, it means "messenger."

> Embrace it .... rather than resist it
> Allow it .... instead of control it
> Bless it .... don't judge it
> Send it love .... not hate

When it hits you upside the noggin, ask, "Why are you here?" Then bless it, thank it and you shall no longer feel the need to condemn it. Illumination comes to the individual seeking to understand the way life is now.

"The fuel source for fear is fear itself!" New quote, hah! Okay, here we are at the ultimate conceptional purpose of these writings. "THE ULTIMATE PERCEPTION."

We gave the Universal Source of all that is a name, and as we so applied it, we created long-term separation in our consciousness. There's more to it. That aforementioned God entity, the one desirous of control, well, He helped us select a good title from his supernatural library of vibrations and frequencies. Of course, He selected the highest of all audible vibrations, man's best friend... spelled backwards. The same has sustained the existence of the Bible throughout history because this word is written in it 4,332 times.

Now let me share a few facts with you. As you know by now, if you read from the front of the book, spoken words carry power. It takes seventy-two muscles to utter one from your lips; each one creates 270 hp. Man's best friend, spelled in reverse order, GOD, creates eighty-six billion cycles per second. This empowered the one who sought to control and rule us each time we uttered it in reference toward an exterior source. Is this making sense, at least in a general way to you, whether or not you believe the seemingly far-fetched nature of the stories underlying the content?

Now, this is not to say don't use the word God. Use it by all means, but as you do, don't place the image of "A God" in your MIND somewhere else, maybe later. Bring this awesome power back to its original source within you, within every cell of you. Are you not the carrying temple of the Lord God?

If you are uncomfortable at first calling yourself such an awesome resounding frequency of hidden power, then open the book and read it to yourself, Psalms 46:10, "Be still and know that 'I AM' God." Anything you resonate toward, with a limiting intent, that is less than perfect, so shall you be. "Be ye perfect even as your Father is in heaven." "He that hath it shall be added," a constructive, creative momentum. Remember who you are, be still and know. Remember who you are, be still and know. Remember who you are, be still and know.

Go to your heart center and head center (third eye) in your meditations, daily. It's time to re-connect with the "God I AM" that you are.

You may have met or overheard someone mention they are looking for a soul mate, or more properly, seeking their twin flame. OKAY, here's ULTIMATE in all perceptions: GOD IS MY TWIN FLAME!

As we assist in perception clearing, feel how you perceive this: Unlike popular belief, could there be something else that humans have backwards besides the spelling of man's best friend? Man was created in the image of God, by God; or was God created in the image of man, by man. Anyway you believe it to be, God is my twin flame, as He is yours.

Here I rest my case because it is in the book. Oh yeah 'tis, I looked it up. Genesis 1:27, "So God created man in His own image, in the image of God created He him; male and female created He them." Of course I took the liberty to look up how Mr. Webster describes the word image. IMAGE: "exact likeness." So now let me ask you, who is your twin flame? So who ya' gonna' call? The one you met at the club? Where ya' gonna' look? God is an indoor kinda' guy!

When you come to this realization, you will stop looking in all the wrong places for love. Your answers are not outside yourself, they come from where truth has always come—from the kingdom within you. No more need for institutions to direct your decision-making. Emerson said, "The difficulty is, we do not make a world of our own, but fall into institutions already made." Organized religion has not the answers to your quest, it's not theirs, it's yours. The way to re-member who you are is through no other way but self-realization.

For this to unfold, you must be the one to stimulate the inner forces. As you get fixed in and continue to use this awesome pres-ence, you will gradually increase its flow to and through you until you realize that each time you move your body, each breath you inhale, each beat of your heart is, in fact, God living through you.

Does your Toyota drive around without a source behind the wheel? Of course not, nor does your body sustain one moment of life lest the great central sun, most high living God, Almighty "I AM" Pres-ence, Christ self is plugged into the heart of it. There's more to the ultimate perception. The God "I AM," you are, gave its outermost expression (you, the ego) a special going-away-from-home gift. Amnesia! You see, God is experiencing six billion ways in which to create on this gorgeous planet earth. This amnesia process, to His divided fragmentational selves, is how He obtains to higher levels of creativity. It is this memory check that makes you feel as a (separate-to-others) individual. Now, feeling this way influences you to create your own world, your way. As you think up new ways to co-create, they are downloaded into the great "IBM" within. Infinite as it may seem, all universe knows to do is grow, no matter how big or small it becomes, it just keeps on becoming more. Some call this "change."

Now, if at any time, you desire to remember who you are, you must apply for amnesia reversal. One request won't cut the mustard. There be many effective methods; but with any of them, you must be determined. When you decide you want to once again be fully conscious of being God/Goddess, you (ego) must override what you (God "I AM") gave you, from your own request, before you decided on this lowered density vibration we title third-dimension. When will you be coming home?

You can never remember who you really are unless you challenge the human masses and "mass" conductors that continue to stimulate this planet with the ignorance of illusion through imagination of appearance and the dead-end limitations you get stuck with because of it.

It is imbedded in us not to overstep our boundaries. Who's boundaries are they? Who creates them? Are they something you wish to claim ownership to? All circumstance that creates limits must be challenged by you.

Upcoming grand perception. They ask Jesus, "Who sent you?" He said, "I AM." There is power in these two words. Use them, followed by what you desire to be, have, or do. This term will keep you in the now, which is the only "time" Universe ever has, and ever will have.

Prepare your minds and hearts to receive some astonishing new insights on your planet soon, real soon! Use Divine Love toward all of it. Turn your mind to open. Set your own barometer and exercise some of these new psychologies. Keep in mind "they," through li'l alter ego, wish to keep you confused so "they" will retain all the little channels you bring them for their own expression. Yes, use you! Step out of the jar they conditioned you in.

True story: There was an experiment done where some students at a university discovered that when they put certain fleas in a jar, they jumped out. Isn't that amazing? Makes you feel like Einstein is performing. Oh wait, there's more. When they put a lid on the jar and left it for some time, they noticed that the fleas were initially jumping to the lid, but after getting thumped on the head enough, they began to jump just high enough so that they would not hit the lid. When the lid was removed, they continued to jump just short of the top and never again jumped high enough to escape. They all died in the open jar. This is how we have been conditioned. It's time to jump out of our jar. It's time to remember who we are.

Here's another perception-clearing truth. These same students set some caterpillars on the rim of a bowl. They crawled around and around and around until they starved to death. They confused activity for accomplishment. The interesting thing here, is that their favorite food was inches away in the center of the bowl, no lids.

The food—your daily bread, spiritual nourishment—is always in your bowl, body, temple, heart, and mind. It is your choice to reach into it. Is this just another book? How about the last one you read and the next? Is there a message here for you? The book is in your eyes, is it not? Whose eyes are they, really? The real you doesn't see with your eyes but through them.

How about the casual statements from friends and strangers that seem to keep coming back to mind so often? Is *The Celestine Prophecy* just someone's fantasy? The Universe provides in perfect order. Do we receive in the same? The way you clean out the closet is to go into it and remove the outdated stuff for what awaits you, to be experienced by you. Make space for the new to come to you. Take a Fung Shui class or read a book about it. Know that the house in which you live is symbolic of the body in which you live. Observe all signs and messages that appear to you outside and more important, the ones that nudge you from within.

If you do not know who God is, how can you use His gifts? When you realize it is God doing the living through one of His many bodies, then you may extend salvation to another through example.

Brothers and sisters, hear me say, "You are right, smack dab in the center of a very important to you truth, ETERNITY." You always have been here, now, and so shall you always be, no matter the area of the universe or dimension therein. The universe will always be in the center of its ETERNAL "NOW."

The end of time as we know it, is approaching nonstop. It's time for perception change. Eartheans, get on the boat now, get in the vibration of D-I-V-I-N-E L-O-V-E for all of it. Love it all, now! Here comes a major grand perception. Do you know what keeps Lucifer hangin' around, alive and well? Your HATE for him and your FEAR of him. I wouldn't worry about it because worry, like hurry, is just another one of his many life-sustaining fuels.

Talk about major grand perceptions, turn up your five sensory perception for a moment and perceive this. Those of you applying or awaiting the usage of your sixth sense; the grand total of this new perception, includes fifty-two senses. To elucidate or conceptualize this fact in a third dimension or density awareness, through a meager five senses, may be to say the least, challenging.

IN FULL CONSCIOUSNESS, THE MOST ULTIMATE OF ALL PERCEPTIONS, IS THE ONE WHEN YOU REMEMBER WHO YOU ARE. Ask yourself daily, "Who am I, really?" Get fixed in self-inquiry. This is how the great ones remember who they are.

"IF YOU HAVE SEEN ME YOU HAVE SEEN THE FATHER."

"I AND THE FATHER ARE ONE."

"ALL THINGS THAT THE FATHER HATH ARE MINE."

I intend the meaning of these words to quicken the memory of the reader so you will remember who you are and begin to express the divine plan that, up to this now moment of time, has awaited patiently your allowance and acceptance. I wisheth that you prosper and have life abundantly. The choice is within your next decision. Make it the highest one available.

If you think in any way I've made fun of the ascended masters, cosmic beings, Jesus, God, or the Holy Spirit of God/man in this message, consider this. I've made fun with them of you, or your convictions that they have needs. They have no needs—you do. At least as you so believe, as you let needs override your wants you are blessed with negative emotion. If your focus is on your wants, you are in the flow of Source, therefore you have positive emotion.

The only one who believes in needs is ego.

I BIND THIS BOOK IN THE NAME OF THE ONE WHO GAVE SO MUCH, YET WE UNDERSTOOD SO LITTLE. THE ONE WHO ATTAINED TO THE MOST POWERFUL VIBRATION IN THE SOLAR LOGOS, THE ONE WHO GAVE HIS ALL TO THE LOST SHEEP, HIS CHILDREN HE LOVES SO DEARLY. I SURRENDER THESE WORDS AND TEACHINGS TO THE GREAT WHITE LIGHT OF JESHYAWA BEN JOSEPH, KNOWN TO US AS JESUS CHRIST.

Thank you Jesus. I love you beyond measure. May the "I AM" Christ consciousness come forth in us all, as is the intent of this one who set the example. You are a co-creator with the beloved most high Father Source. God created the earth so as to experience life through her, and through us on her.

You may think that you are not the sole creator of the way your life is just now. Maybe it's true. I have not, the attitude of the want-to-be-right syndrome. I wouldn't argue the point. However, let me ask you, who has the power invested in them to re-create it? Someone else on your behalf? I think not.

Life begins its initial creation always, where the power is that propels it. No matter what country you live in, no matter what big, mean man, woman, parent, or child is assuming control over you or abusing you; all you need do, if your life is not the way you prefer it to be, is to think it, or more properly rethink it, to the way you desire it.

You are living in the freewill zone of the Universe and no-thing may take your freedom of the way in which you think. This is where creation begins. THE POWER IS IN THE THOUGHT.

Each circumstance that arrives in your life today that's not what you prefer, stop, close your eyes, breathe two or three smooth, deep breaths, bless the circumstance, ask how to resolve and understand it. Say THANK YOU and go on to the next step soul brings you to.

As you actually implement the simple procedures in these writings, you will notice proof of their awesome power in re-creating your life within days, no more than weeks. You must understand that simplicity is key in this Universe.

I've conveyed to you many perceptions, grand to ultimate. I will leave you with one final, hopefully lasting, perception. You see, it's not all about what takes place in life, it's all about the way you perceive it. No other can manipulate your perception, it's yours for keeps.

THE IMMACULATE PERCEPTION
Don't ya' know I looked it up?

IMMACULATE:
Having no stain or blemish
Pure
Containing no flaw or error
Spotlessly clean

You are not a body—you live through the body. This is how you obtain knowledge, through experience, on the third dimension and many other dimensions through many other bodies.

YOU ARE SPIRIT!
PERFECT DIVINE SPIRIT!

You may wonder where some of this information came from. Some of it from some heavy meditations or should I say "Light" meditations. It would take a book in itself to give the details. However, I will share where this part came from. You should find it quite interesting.

I was new in the field of public speaking. Through a dear friend of mine named Barbara, I met a dear friend of hers. She asked that I not mention her name, but I will give her address, phone number and where she works. Only jesting my children, only jesting.

This wonderful lady owns some properties she rents out for the exclusive purpose of spiritual or religious groups to hold services. I have given seminars for groups there several times. There is a reason why I share this about her.

I was driving along with her and Barbara one morning as she related her experience. She recalls it word for word. If you can call it words. I will do the best I can.

She said, "One night I couldn't sleep so I got out of bed and went into the kitchen. I noticed it was 3:00 AM. I sat in a comfortable chair and decided I would do a mantra. I began to chant the words, 'Be still and know that I AM God.' After about thirty minutes, I shot straight up out of my body. I heard a loud, thundering crack, then another and another. I soon realized these cracking sounds as the breaking through into higher dimensions. I experienced seven total and recognized it as meaning I was on the seventh plane of awareness.

"This was the most profound experience, by far, I'd ever had. I received an extremely crystal-clear message there. It was not only audio sound or just sight or even just telepathic, but with perfection of all knowingness. In words, it is best transcribed thusly: 'YOU ARE IMMACULATE CONCEPTION OF PERFECTION. YOU ARE PURE, UNSTAINED, UNBLEMISHED, PERFECT DIVINE SPIRIT! NOW, GO BACK, SHARE THIS WITH THEM ALL.' "

That is as accurate as I recall what she told me and it may be exact because it left a deep impression on me. This lady also mentioned that she had this experience via the third eye, "pituitary gland." Here's an affirmation that you may use to remember who you are:

"I AM CHRIST, son of the most high, living God."

"All things that the Father hath are mine." John 16:15

This is how to reveal yourself to yourself. KEEP YOUR ATTENTION EVER and FOREVER fixed on "The Almighty 'I AM' Presence" within and just above you. Pour out your gratitude to this one and only source of allness. "Let Thy will be mine," "Let Thy will be mine," "Let Thy will be mine." Ask the ascended masters to illumine your consciousness in the Light of the Cosmic Christ. Now go bless someone whom you judge as not deserving of it and observe your world begin to shift.

Till we meet in another NOW moment.

"I AM."

ABOUT THE AUTHOR:
DAVID PORTER

Namasté: The God "I AM" in me salutes
the God "I AM" in you.

When David was 20 years of age, an acquaintance gave him a book titled
ESP by Harold Sherman. This was David's introduction to metaphysical
or spiritual concepts other than the previous fundamental belief systems
of the established religious order.

David attuned to the information of this "God-source" concept instantly
through these more un-common sense ways of being explained. It was
truth and he knew it. It rang so loud and clear for him as truth that his
thirst for it became unquenchable. The knowledge, the wisdom, the truth
of our being became his chosen life path.

On his quest, the information through numerology was taught to him
that he, in fact, is under the direct influence of the number 7 as a life path
lesson number. Deriving from his date of birth, the 7 represents the seeker
of wisdom, knowledge, intuition, inspiration, philosophy, and mysticism.
His 25 years of study has become his message unveiled to those who, like
him, know there is more to the mysteries of life, money, power, God, Christ,
religion that most understand.

David moved to Sedona, Arizona in 1997 on his birthday, June 10th where
he completed the writing for this book. He currently resides in Sedona.

Seminars and workshops on this material
with David are available for your group
or organization. Call or write for further
information.